EASY EATS

EASY EATS

Quick · Tasty · Vegan

CANDICE HUTCHINGS

Robert
ROSE

Library and Archives Canada Cataloguing in Publication

Title: The edgy veg : easy eats : quick, tasty, vegan / Candice Hutchings.
Names: Hutchings, Candice, 1988- author.
Description: Includes index.
Identifiers: Canadiana 20220142068 | ISBN 9780778807032 (hardcover)
Subjects: LCSH: Vegan cooking. | LCSH: Quick and easy cooking. | LCGFT: Cookbooks.
Classification: LCC TX837 .H885 2022 | DDC 641.5/6362—dc23

Disclaimer

The recipes in this book have been carefully tested by our kitchen and our tasters. To the best of our knowledge, they are safe and nutritious for ordinary use and users. For those people with food or other allergies, or who have special food requirements or health issues, please read the suggested contents of each recipe carefully and determine whether or not they may create a problem for you. All recipes are used at the risk of the consumer.

We cannot be responsible for any hazards, loss or damage that may occur as a result of any recipe use.

For those with special needs, allergies, requirements or health problems, in the event of any doubt, please contact your medical adviser prior to the use of any recipe.

At the time of publication, all URLs referenced link to existing websites. Robert Rose Inc. is not responsible for maintaining, and does not endorse the content of, any website or content not created by Robert Rose Inc.

COVER DESIGN: Naomi MacDougall
INTERIOR DESIGN & PRODUCTION: Kevin Cockburn/PageWave Graphics Inc.
COVER PHOTOGRAPHY: Mollie Pie
BACK COVER & INTERIOR PHOTOGRAPHY: Brilynn Ferguson
FOOD & PROP STYLING: Candice Hutchings, Charlotte Langley and Adam Ward
EDITORS: Meredith Dees and Michelle Meade
COPYEDITOR: Judy Phillips
PROOFREADER: Kelly Jones
INDEXER: Gillian Watts
ICONS: © Getty Images

The publisher gratefully acknowledges the financial support of our publishing program by the Government of Canada through the Canada Book Fund.

Canadä

Published by Robert Rose Inc.
120 Eglinton Avenue East, Suite 800, Toronto, Ontario, Canada M4P 1E2
Tel: (416) 322-6552 Fax: (416) 322-6936
www.robertrose.ca

Printed and bound in China

1 2 3 4 5 6 7 8 9 ESP 30 29 28 27 26 25 24 23 22

TO MY INCREDIBLE
EDGY VEG TEAM: RYAN,
MOLLY, ANTHONY AND ERIC.
THANK YOU FOR HELPING
ME MAKE MY WILDEST
DREAMS COME TRUE.

TABLE OF CONTENTS

THINGS THAT MAKE YOU GO MMMMAINS

SIDE HUSTLE

POTENT POTABLES

SUGAR HIGH

INTRODUCTION

AND WE'RE BACK!

Welcome to the second season of *The Edgy Veg*! So many things have changed since season one. Chances are you belong in one of two categories: (1) you're one of the huge fans of *The Edgy Veg* who have been begging me for the better part of three years to write another book or (2) you were intrigued by a rad-looking cookbook with easy vegan recipes. In any case, allow me to reintroduce myself.

I'm Candice, that vegan with the fiery red hair from YouTube. Over 10 years ago, I decided to take a dive face-first into an animal-free lifestyle. But, being of the cause-driven millennial generation that I am, I couldn't just eat plants and live my life — no, I had to make a career out of it. Voilà! The Edgy Veg blog, YouTube channel and, subsequently, the cookbook were born.

If you've been following along since the first book came out, skip ahead to the next paragraph while I recap for the newbies everything that has changed recently. And I mean A LOT has changed. I left my marriage, ran away to Italy *(because who doesn't want to drown their sorrows in spaghetti and wine?)* and weathered a toxic AF divorce. Like my mother before me, I came out the other side stronger than ever. I've spent the last three years rebuilding my broken business and hiring an incredible team of people, who have since become close friends. I am so proud of what we are achieving.

Big changes, of course, are often met with resistance, and for me that manifested as chronic anxiety and depression. It was a dark time, and I didn't handle it well, but day by day I learned to take care of myself and find joy again in the things I once loved: dancing, cooking, hosting girls' nights. Heck, I figured out how to care for myself so effectively, I even adopted two more special-needs fur babies! [Insert here mental picture of the cutest little blind and deaf dog that barks like a chicken and the sweetest geriatric. *Hi Kevin and Mr. Frederickson!*]

This book is the byproduct of every lesson I had to learn. It includes all the no-fuss recipes that kept me nourished on my journey back to myself, and the take-no-shit advice I now live by. In many ways, food was my medicine.

Writing it saved me from COVID-19 boredom, brought me closer to my chosen family and nourished every fiber of my being.

These pages are the simpler everyday little sister to the foundational carnivore-approved vegan recipes of the first book. And like most cookbooks, this one is full of recipes. Unlike most cookbooks, however, these recipes don't sacrifice creativity or bold flavor for ease or time. Not only will they save you energy for whatever life tosses your way, they take the guesswork and, well, work out of preparing tasty meals. *Do you really want to spend every night for the rest of your living days figuring out what to cook for dinner?* Yeah, neither do I. In these pages, you will find vegan food built differently. Food that will satiate every craving. Food that will make your soul sing. This includes everything from delicious recipes to impress your latest fling to tasty one-pot dinners when you've got a case of the Mondays. I'm serving you drool-worthy and lightning-fast appetizers and no-fuss desserts for when you need a sweet fix in a hurry. Flip to any page and you'll find a great-tasting recipe that can be made in less than 45 minutes. (I even snuck in a naughty libation or two for when you need a hug from something alcohol based.) Ingredient lists include only those ingredients you can easily find at your local grocery store. No more backbreaking, long-haul, wallet-robbing treks to the fancy health food store for you, honey! In no time at all you will be serving up mains with attitude and some cheeky sides.

"But Candice," you might ask, "do I have to be vegan or know how to cook to use this book?" Heck no! This book is for anyone who feels edgy by nature — for those of us just trying to make it through this world doing good while feeling good through eating good: the budding entrepreneur, the busy activist, the parent with a side hustle and anyone who cooks a nice dinner one day and then has two bowls of Froot Loops the next. Whether life throws you lemons or tosses you a bone, we all need to eat — preferably really tasty food — and this book's got your back!

— *Candice*

WHAT'S IN THE BOOK?

THIS BOOK IS FOR EVERYONE.

Whether you're a new vegan, long-time vegan, a vegetarian, pescatarian, flexitarian or don't define your eating habits at all — these recipes are simply for tasty food (that doesn't happen to contain meat or dairy)! Make one recipe if you're feeling lazy, or mix and match to create a two- to four-course feast that cooks in no time at all. Each recipe is designed to take 45 minutes or less of active cooking time, with easy-to-find ingredients that require minimal prep.

I said this in my first book, and I'll say it again: **read the recipe, *then* cook**. This is the best piece of advice I've learned over years of cooking not only my own but everyone else's recipes, too. By reading the recipe through first, you'll know exactly what you need, what you're doing and what other tasks you can do while you're cooking. Got 20 minutes to spare while your soup simmers? Start setting the table, wash some dishes or get going on dessert! My recipes also highlight what tools to grab. I like to have everything on my counter ready to go, so that I'm not looking for anything right when I need it, only to find my dirty blender in the dishwasher.

HACK ITS!

In many of my recipes you'll find a little *Hack It!* note. It may be an additional tip or trick for simplifying the recipe even further, or a flavor variation you can try to change it up.

ICONS

Cookbooks can be intimidating, so I've included four icons to help you find the perfect recipes for whatever you're craving.

 15 MINUTES OR LESS: Do you really need me to explain this one to you?

 ONE POT/ONE PAN: One recipe in one pot or one pan means fewer dishes to clean up. You're welcome.

 GLUTEN-FREE: If you are celiac or just prefer to avoid gluten, look out for this one. Along with the GF-specific recipes I identify, you will notice that I also often lay out gluten-free alternatives for you in the *Hack It!* sections of many recipes. Celiacs: Make sure any alternative I call out (like cornstarch) is made in a GF facility.

 GREAT FOR ENTERTAINING: Let the food do the talking with these impressive but foolproof crowd-pleasers and potluck-ready dishes.

YOU OUGHTA KNOW

HOW DO I GET AQUAFABA?

Aquafaba is the liquid you find in canned beans. Yup, that liquid you've been draining and dumping down the sink for years makes an excellent egg substitute for cakes, meringues, breadings (for frying) and mousses. Because of its neutral flavor, the liquid from chickpeas is the one used most often, but you can also use the liquid from white beans, as well as the liquid from black beans for darker baked items like brownies.

You can get aquafaba in one of two ways. **(1)** Drain a can of chickpeas (or beans of choice) and reserve the liquid. (Please note there've been some concerns about chemical contaminations from cans, so I would recommend buying BPA-free canned chickpeas.) **(2)** Cook your own chickpeas (or beans of choice) and reserve the cooking liquid. (This method is more time-consuming and, in my opinion, less reliable.)

SO ABOUT KALA NAMAK . . .

Kala namak is a kiln-fired rock salt used in a lot of South Asian cuisine. It has a very strong sulfur-like smell, and the taste is similar to eggs. It is traditionally used as a condiment in cooking or added to salads and savory snacks. In the recipes in this book, it's used mainly to add an eggy flavor to our vegan dishes. If you don't have it, don't fear! Use sea salt instead.

WHEN A RECIPE SAYS "CASHEWS, SOAKED . . ."

Easy peasy . . . all it requires is a little bit of time management. Soaking cashews overnight is ideal for creating the perfect neutral cashew-free flavor. Simply place raw cashews in a mason jar or bowl and fill with enough water to cover completely. Soak in the fridge for at least 6 hours or up to 24 hours. When you are ready to use, drain the cashews and give them a very thorough rinse.

Pressed for time? No problem! For a quick method, simply pour boiling water over the cashews and soak for 1 hour. When you are ready to use, drain and rinse. It won't garner the exact same results, but it's close enough not to be a problem.

HOW THE HECK DO YOU PRESS TOFU?

Pressing tofu is one of the easiest ways to level up your dish. During the process, excess liquid is removed, which will allow the tofu to get extra crispy when you bake or fry it. It will also help the tofu soak up lots of the tasty marinades. There are two main methods:

Using a tofu press: place your tofu in the press, secure and let stand for 15 minutes.

Pressing tofu by hand: Wrap your tofu in a clean dish towel and place it on a cutting board or large plate. Carefully cover it with something heavy, like a cast-iron skillet or some hardcover books, and let it do its thing for 15 minutes.

KITCHEN STAPLES

~~~~~~~~~~

The whole point of this book is to help you cook mouthwatering delicious meals while keeping things quick and easy — your pantry included. A lot of vegan and vegetarian cookbooks give you long lists of funny-sounding and hard-to-find specialty ingredients — I'm not going to do that to you. Instead, here's a list of a few key items you will come across over and over again as you cook your way through this book. Keep these on hand and you'll always be armed and ready to head into flavor town.

FRIDGE
- Butter (dairy-free)
- Mayo (egg-free)
- Soy milk (unsweetened)
- Tofu (firm, medium-firm, soft)
- Veggie ground beef
- Yogurt (plain dairy-free)

PANTRY
- Agave
- Beans (white, such as cannellini)
- Cashews (raw)
- Chickpeas (canned; for aquafaba, see page 15)
- Coconut milk (full fat)
- Coconut oil (refined)
- Cornstarch
- Flour (unbleached all-purpose)
- Liquid smoke
- Maple syrup (pure)
- Marshmallows (gelatin-free)
- Nutritional yeast
- Olive oil
- Pasta (dried; such as penne, spaghetti or rotini)
- Sesame oil (toasted)
- Sesame seeds (raw)
- Sugar (organic granulated)
- Tahini
- Tamari or soy sauce
- Tomatoes (canned; crushed or diced)
- Vinegar (apple cider, seasoned rice)

SPICES & SEASONINGS
- Black pepper
- Bouillon (no-chicken, no-beef or vegetable)
- Broth (no-chicken or vegetable)
- Cayenne pepper
- Cinnamon (ground)
- Cumin (ground)
- Dill (dried)
- Garlic powder
- Italian seasoning
- Kala namak (page 15)
- Onion powder
- Oregano (dried)
- Paprika
- Parsley (dried)
- Red pepper flakes
- Sea salt
- Taco seasoning
- Thyme (dried)
- Turmeric (ground)

TOOLS OF THE TRADE
- Blender (high-powered)
- Can opener
- Colander
- Cutting board
- Knives (sharp!)
- Measuring cups and spoons
- Mixing bowls (S, M, L)
- Parchment paper
- Pots and pans (S, M, L)
- Rimmed baking sheets
- Stand mixer or electric hand mixer
- Whisk

HELPFUL ADDITIONS TO MAKE LIFE EASIER
- 12-cup muffin tin
- Fine-mesh sieve
- Food processor
- Mortar and pestle
- Silicone baking mats (see opposite)
- Spatulas
- Tofu press
- Wire racks
- Wooden spoons
- Zester or microplane

SILICONE BAKING MATS

Throughout this book, you are asked to line a baking sheet with parchment paper. But if you have a silicone baking mat, you can use it instead. (I do.) Silicone baking mats are made from food-grade silicone and have a nonstick surface. They can be used exactly like parchment paper in baking or roasting, with one key difference: they're reusable! They come in various sizes and shapes, they are super easy to clean and, most importantly, they are better for the environment than single-use parchment paper. The choice is yours.

Okay, veggie babies, let's get cooking!

BREAK

because it's the most

THE

important meal of the day

FAST

'brāk \ <u>th</u>ə \ fast *(noun)*

1. **Break:** pausing an action or work. **Fast:** as in not eating for a long period of time. *"Wow, I must have slept for 14 hours! Time to break the fast like a gosh-darn champion! Pass the muffins."*

2. A meal that is usually eaten in the morning, sometimes served in bed, often with a cocktail. *"I don't think I've ever drunk champagne before breakfast. With breakfast on several occasions, but never before . . ."*

~~~~~~~~~~~~~~~~~~~~~~~~~~~~~~~~~~~~~~~

Breakfast food is totally on another level. I don't know why, but when it comes to our morning meal, we tend to throw all the rules out the window. Is it sweet savory or savory? Large or small? Healthy or decadent? Who cares? It's breakfast, where desserts are considered a main. Are you in the mood for something sweet like French toast covered in syrup and whipped cream? Fantastic! Or perhaps you're longing for something like tacos, so make it brunch with some eggs? Right on! Those are exactly the types of creations found in this chapter. Both are enticing and acceptable options to help you seize the day. Don't forget your coffee!

NOT-SO-BASIC BETCH TOAST 5 WAYS

Some toasts have gotten a bad rap lately. Personally, I think it's because the boomers blame the "pretentious" avocado toast for everything. But that doesn't mean we need to hate on all toasts! I mean, why is toast just SO MUCH better than bread? It has so many functions: a breakfast for busy betches; a peace offering for when *you* weren't wrong but you want to be the bigger person and start the day off on the right foot; or a quick and easy appetizer for when someone just "stops by." *Ewwww, who just stops by?!*

HOW TO TOAST A BAGUETTE: Preheat the oven to 400°F (200°C). Cut baguette diagonally in ¼-inch (0.5 cm) thick slices. Arrange the slices in a single layer on a rimmed baking sheet lined with parchment paper and brush lightly with olive oil. Bake for 10 to 15 minutes, turning halfway, until lightly toasted. Top with any of these combinations and enjoy!

AVOCADO CAPRESE

SERVES 2

It's like avocado toast, but with a tomato glow-up!

⅔ **cup (150 mL)** balsamic vinegar

2 ripe avocados, mashed

4 toasted bread slices or 16 toasted baguette slices (see box, above)

2 plum (Roma) tomatoes, chopped

Sea salt and freshly ground black pepper

4 fresh basil leaves, chopped

1   In a small saucepan over low heat, bring balsamic vinegar to a simmer, whisking occasionally, until vinegar has reduced to ¼ cup (60 mL). It can burn easily, so watch closely. Remove from heat and let cool while you prepare the rest of the recipe.

2   Spread mashed avocado on toasts and top with some tomatoes. Season to taste with sea salt and pepper and drizzle with the balsamic reduction. Garnish with basil.

HACK IT!

Use leftover balsamic reduction in salads or drizzle over bruschetta, grilled veggies and even ice cream or fruit.

NOT A PB&J

SERVES 2

She may look like a PB&J, but think of her as the more grown-up, slightly bohemian older sister. She's savory with a hint of tart sweetness . . .

¾ **cup (175 mL)** tahini

4 toasted bread slices or 16 toasted baguette slices (see box, opposite)

½ **cup (125 mL)** fresh raspberries, mashed

Pure maple syrup

Sesame seeds (optional)

1 Spread tahini on toasts. Top with mashed raspberries. Drizzle with maple syrup and garnish with a sprinkle of sesame seeds (if using).

ONIONS 'N' HUMMUS

SERVES 2

These aesthetic toasts are a delicious way to get your protein and greens before 9 a.m.!

1 tbsp (15 mL) olive oil

½ small red onion, thinly sliced

¾ **cup (175 mL)** prepared hummus

4 toasted bread slices or 16 toasted baguette slices (see box, opposite)

Sea salt and freshly ground black pepper

½ **cup (125 mL)** arugula

1 In a small skillet, heat olive oil over medium heat. Add onion and cook, stirring occasionally, for 7 to 10 minutes, until soft and slightly browned. Set aside.

2 Spread hummus on toasts. Top with sautéed onion. Sprinkle with sea salt and pepper to taste and finish with arugula.

LE PETITE STRAWBERRY CHEESECAKE

SERVES 2

When I make this, I instantly transform into the main character of a French film. *Bonjour!* Opulence is served!

1 cup (250 mL) chopped fresh strawberries

1 tbsp (15 mL) freshly squeezed lemon juice

¾ cup (175 mL) dairy-free cream cheese, softened

4 toasted bread slices or 16 toasted baguette slices (see box, page 22)

1 tsp (5 mL) grated lemon zest (optional)

1. In a small bowl, toss the strawberries with lemon juice. Set aside.

2. Spread dairy-free cream cheese on toasts. Top with strawberry mixture and garnish with lemon zest (if using).

SALTED NO-TELLA CRUNCH

SERVES 2

I mean, who didn't grow up thinking Nutella on toast was part of a well-balanced breakfast?! LOL. Add some salt and fancy cut almonds and you have yourself an elegant treat.

¾ cup (175 mL) No-Tella (page 26)

4 toasted bread slices or 16 toasted baguette slices (see box, page 22)

2 tbsp (30 mL) slivered almonds

Flakey sea salt

1. Spread No-Tella on toasts. Top with slivered almonds and a light sprinkle of flakey sea salt.

NO-TELLA

Listen sister, you can't make everyone happy. You're not a jar of Nutella. But you can make my version and try!

- **RIMMED BAKING SHEET**
- **2-CUP (500 ML) JAR WITH LID (OPTIONAL)**
- **FOOD PROCESSOR OR HIGH-POWERED BLENDER**

8 oz (250 g) raw hazelnuts (roughly 1½ cups/375 mL)

½ cup (125 mL) confectioners' (icing) sugar

⅓ cup (75 mL) unsweetened cocoa powder

3 tbsp (45 mL) refined coconut oil, softened

1 tsp (5 mL) vanilla extract

⅛ tsp (0.5 mL) sea salt

1 Preheat the oven to 350°F (180°C).

2 Spread hazelnuts on the baking sheet. Bake in the preheated oven for 5 to 8 minutes, flipping halfway, until hazelnuts are lightly colored and fragrant and the skins are cracked.

3 Carefully transfer hot hazelnuts to a jar or sealable container, seal with the lid and shake to remove the skins.

4 Place peeled hazelnuts in the food processor (reserving jar). Process for 3 to 5 minutes, until very smooth.

5 Add confectioners' sugar, cocoa, coconut oil, vanilla and sea salt; process for about 10 seconds, until smooth.

6 Transfer to a jar and let mixture cool, uncovered, completely. The No-Tella will keep for up to 2 weeks in the fridge.

PUMPKIN SCONE LOVE

MAKES 8 SCONES

It's fall. You're rocking an infinity scarf and sniffing a spiced autumnal candle. You've got your PSL in one hand and a coveted pumpkin scone in the other . . . oh, wait. No, you don't! They're not vegan, and youuuuuu can't have one. I can't have the Regina George of the decorative pumpkin cohort kicking you out of this year's "Welcome Fall" Insta pic. (How many pictures of dark beige nails and fallen leaves is too many? Asking for a friend . . .) No worries, I got you, boo. I've veganized this Starbucks fave so you could have a treat to go with your yuppie crack.

- **STAND MIXER (OPTIONAL)**
- **RIMMED BAKING SHEET LINED WITH PARCHMENT PAPER**

1 cup (250 mL) canned pumpkin purée

3 tbsp (45 mL) aquafaba (page 15)

¼ cup (60 mL) unsweetened soy milk (approx.), divided

2 tsp (10 mL) apple cider vinegar

2 tsp (10 mL) vanilla extract

3 cups (750 mL) unbleached all-purpose flour (approx.)

¾ cup (175 mL) packed brown sugar

1 tbsp (15 mL) ground ginger

1 tbsp (15 mL) pumpkin pie spice

2½ tsp (12 mL) baking powder

1 tsp (5 mL) baking soda

1 tsp (5 mL) ground cinnamon

½ tsp (2 mL) sea salt

6 to 8 tbsp (90 to 120 mL) cold dairy-free butter

½ cup (125 mL) confectioners' (icing) sugar, sifted

1. Preheat the oven to 400°F (200°C).

2. In a medium bowl, whisk together pumpkin purée, aquafaba, 2 tbsp (30 mL) soy milk, apple cider vinegar and vanilla until well combined. Set aside.

3. In the bowl of the stand mixer fitted with the paddle attachment (or in a large bowl using a fork), combine flour, brown sugar, ginger, pumpkin pie spice, baking powder, baking soda, cinnamon and sea salt. Add dairy-free butter to flour mixture, 1 tbsp (15 mL) at a time, and beat or stir until the mixture resembles coarse crumbs.

4. Now knead the dough! Add the wet mixture to the stand mixer (or large bowl); beat or stir until the dough just comes together. If needed, sprinkle in 1 tbsp (15 mL) flour at a time until the dough is wet but not sticky.

5. On a lightly floured surface, shape dough into a 1½-inch (4 cm) thick circle. Using a sharp knife, cut the dough into eight wedges.

6. Transfer to the prepared baking sheet, spacing about 1 inch (2.5 cm) apart. Bake in the preheated oven for 15 to 20 minutes, until golden brown.

7. Meanwhile, in a small bowl, whisk together confectioners' sugar and the remaining 2 tbsp (30 mL) soy milk until smooth. You want a thick but pourable glaze. If the glaze is too thick, add more soy milk 1 tbsp (15 mL) at a time until you are able to drizzle it.

8. Remove scones from the oven and let cool on the baking sheet for 5 minutes. Transfer scones to a wire rack and drizzle with the glaze. Store in a container at room temperature for up to 2 days or in the fridge for 5 days.

HOUSTON! WE'VE GOT HUEVOS!

SERVES 4

Ya know that saying "Everything but the kitchen sink"? Well, this breakfast recipe has all the staples of a Tex-Mex meal in one skillet — and you can easily swap things out or in depending on what you have on hand. Don't have a green bell pepper? Use yellow! Out of black beans but have pinto? Fab! Even the method of eating it is loosey-goosey. Want it in a taco? Fantastic! More of a burrito chick? Do that!

2 packages (each 16 oz/450 g) medium-firm tofu, drained and crumbled

¼ cup (60 mL) nutritional yeast

1 tsp (5 mL) ground turmeric

½ tsp (2 mL) kala namak or sea salt

1 tsp (5 mL) coconut oil

1 small onion, diced

2 garlic cloves, minced

1 jalapeño pepper, seeded and chopped (optional)

1 tsp (5 mL) ground cumin

1 tsp (5 mL) chili powder

1 can (14 oz/398 mL) black beans, drained

2 plum (Roma) tomatoes, diced

1 green bell pepper, diced

1 red bell pepper, diced

½ tsp (2 mL) sea salt

¼ tsp (1 mL) freshly ground black pepper

½ cup (125 mL) tomato salsa

ACCOMPANIMENTS

16 small tortillas (see *Hack It!*)

Tortilla chips

2 ripe avocados, mashed

¼ cup (60 mL) fresh cilantro, chopped

1 lime, cut into wedges

Hot sauce

1 Heat a large skillet over medium-high heat. Add tofu, nutritional yeast, turmeric and kala namak; cook, stirring constantly, for 7 to 10 minutes, until the liquid from the tofu has evaporated. Transfer mixture to a bowl (reserving skillet). Cover to keep warm.

2 In the reserved skillet, heat coconut oil over medium-high heat. Add onion, garlic, jalapeño (if using), cumin and chili powder; cook, stirring occasionally, for 3 to 5 minutes, until onion is translucent and spices are fragrant. Add black beans, tomatoes, bell peppers, sea salt and black pepper; bring to a boil. Reduce heat to medium and simmer, stirring occasionally, for about 10 minutes, until peppers are tender and beans are heated through.

3 Meanwhile, wrap tortillas in damp paper towel. Microwave on High in 15-second intervals until warm. Remove from microwave and wrap in a clean dish towel to keep warm until ready to serve.

4 Move peppers mixture over to one side of the skillet. Add tofu back to the skillet and heat for 3 minutes, or until warmed. Remove the skillet from the heat and dig a little hole in the center of the mixture to make a home for your salsa.

5 Place the skillet on a trivet in the center of the table, surrounded by the accompaniments. Treat each plate as a blank canvas — allow each guest to create their own brunch adventure by turning this skillet into tacos or haystacks (see *Hack It!*). They could also use tortilla chips as utensils. The topping possibilities are endless!

HACK IT!

For incredible burritos, just use large tortillas instead of small.

HACK IT!

Hey Candice! What's a haystack?! Well, it's a mix between a taco salad and nachos . . . kinda. Pile chips onto a plate and then smother them with your bean mixture, tofu eggs and tasty accompaniments.

GARLICKY GREEN EGGS

SERVES 4

Tofu scramble dyed green with spinach and garlic? I would eat them in a house, I would eat them with a mouse. I would eat them here or there, I would eat them anywhere! I really do love garlicky green eggs, Sam. I enjoy them even more without the ham!

• HIGH-POWERED BLENDER

½ cup (125 mL) water (approx.)

3 cups (750 mL) chopped spinach, divided

¼ cup (60 mL) nutritional yeast

½ tsp (2 mL) ground turmeric

½ tsp (2 mL) kala namak or sea salt

¼ tsp (1 mL) freshly ground black pepper

½ cube (½ tsp/2 mL) vegetable bouillon

1 tbsp (15 mL) coconut oil

1 small onion, finely chopped

4 garlic cloves, minced

1½ packages (each 16 oz/ 450 g) medium-firm tofu, drained and crumbled

1½ tsp (7 mL) dried dill

½ tsp (2 mL) red pepper flakes

1   In the high-powered blender, combine water, 1 cup (250 mL) spinach, nutritional yeast, turmeric, kala namak, pepper and bouillon; blend on high speed until smooth and pourable. Add more water, 1 tbsp (15 mL) at a time, until it blends easily. Set aside.

2   In a large saucepan, heat coconut oil over medium-high heat. Add onion; cook, stirring occasionally, for 3 to 5 minutes, until translucent. Add garlic; cook for about 2 minutes, until fragrant.

3   Add tofu and increase heat to high; cook for 5 minutes, stirring occasionally, or until the liquid has evaporated.

4   Add spinach mixture and cook, stirring occasionally, for 10 to 12 minutes, until the liquid has evaporated.

5   Add the remaining 2 cups (500 mL) spinach and dill; cook for about 3 minutes, until greens are wilted. Season to taste with kala namak and pepper. Garnish with red pepper flakes.

6   Serve with a side of your favorite vegan bacon or sausage, along with pancakes, buttered toast or waffles. You will love them Sam-I-Am, you will love garlicky green eggs . . . without the ham.

IT'LL MAKE YOU QUAKE, OATMEAL CAKE

SERVES 4

It's unfathomable to me that anyone can enjoy beige, loose slop with cold milk on top. Thus, I did what I do with everything I don't like in my life: *I divorced him . . .* I mean, fixed it! Like your first hookup after a breakup, this hits harder and hotter. The fluffy texture, bursts of blueberry and lemon zip will have you convinced you're eating cake for breakfast.

• HIGH-POWERED BLENDER
• FOUR 1-CUP (250 ML) RAMEKINS

1 cup (250 mL) unsweetened non-dairy milk of choice

2 bananas

1⅓ cups (325 mL) large-flake (old-fashioned) rolled oats

½ cup (125 mL) dairy-free plain yogurt

¼ cup (60 mL) pure maple syrup

1½ tsp (7 mL) vanilla extract

1 tsp (5 mL) baking powder

½ tsp (2 mL) baking soda

½ tsp (2 mL) sea salt

½ cup (125 mL) fresh blueberries, divided

1 tbsp (15 mL) grated lemon zest

¼ cup (60 mL) confectioners' (icing) sugar

2 tbsp (30 mL) freshly squeezed lemon juice

1 Preheat the oven to 400°F (200°C).

2 In the high-powered blender, combine non-dairy milk, bananas, rolled oats, dairy-free yogurt, maple syrup, vanilla, baking powder, baking soda and sea salt; blend on high speed until smooth. Gently stir in ¼ cup (60 mL) blueberries and lemon zest.

3 Transfer to ramekins. Top ramekins with the remaining ¼ cup (60 mL) blueberries.

4 Bake in the preheated oven for 20 minutes, or until a tester inserted into the center comes out clean.

5 Remove from the oven and let stand for 10 minutes. I know they smell incredible, but they are hot AF! Wait the 10 minutes or risk a mouth of lava!

6 Meanwhile, in a small cup or bowl, whisk together confectioners' sugar and lemon juice until smooth. Drizzle some over each cake and serve.

HACK IT!

Swap out the pairing of blueberries and lemon for strawberry and lemon, banana chunks and dairy-free chocolate chips, or apple and walnuts. Or ditch the fruit altogether and toss in the same amount of dairy-free chocolate chips.

HACK IT!

Turn this recipe into mini quiche lorraines by replacing the onion and spinach with ¼ cup (60 mL) chopped vegan bacon, 2 chopped green onions and 1 tbsp (15 mL) chopped flat-leaf (Italian) parsley.

MANY TINY FLORENTINE QUICHES

MAKES 1 DOZEN TINY QUICHES

Listen, I normally don't quiche and tell, but you spent money on this book, so you're entitled to all my secrets. This make-ahead quiche is the perfect plant-based recipe. Why? Well, aside from being my recipe of choice for brunches, showers and parties, it is also undeniably rich while still having a delicate mouthfeel. You know what it is not? A frittata with a crust.

> • **12-CUP MUFFIN TIN**
> • **2 CUPS (500 ML) DRIED BEANS OR CERAMIC BAKING WEIGHTS**
> • **HIGH-POWERED BLENDER**

Twelve 3-inch (7.5 cm) vegan-friendly tart shells, frozen

2 tbsp (30 mL) olive oil, divided

1 small onion, diced

Water

2 cups (500 mL) packed chopped spinach leaves

8 oz (225 g) soft or medium-firm tofu, drained

1 tsp (5 mL) Dijon mustard

2 tbsp (30 mL) nutritional yeast

1 tsp (5 mL) garlic powder

¼ tsp (1 mL) ground turmeric

¼ cup (60 mL) unsweetened soy milk

1½ tbsp (22 mL) rice flour (approx.)

1½ tsp (7 mL) cornstarch

1 cube (1 tsp/5 mL) vegetable bouillon

Kala namak or sea salt

Freshly ground black pepper

5 cherry tomatoes, chopped

1 cup (250 mL) shredded dairy-free Parmesan or mozzarella cheese

1 tsp (5 mL) herbs de provence

¼ tsp (1 mL) ground nutmeg

1. Preheat the oven to 375°F (190°C).

2. Arrange tart shells in muffin cups. Fill each cup with a layer of dried beans or ceramic weights. Bake in the preheated oven for 5 to 10 minutes, until the crust edges are lightly browned. Remove from the oven and let cool while you prepare the rest of the recipe.

3. Meanwhile, in a small saucepan, heat 1 tbsp (15 mL) olive oil over medium-high heat. Add onion; cook, stirring occasionally, for 3 to 5 minutes, until translucent. Remove one-third of the onion and set aside on a plate. Cook the remaining onion, stirring occasionally, for another 7 to 10 minutes, until caramelized. Add 1 tbsp (15 mL) water every 2 minutes if the bottom of the saucepan becomes brown and sticky. Remove the saucepan from the heat and add spinach; stir to combine. Cover with a lid and let stand for 2 to 4 minutes, until wilted. If the spinach is not wilting, add 1 tbsp (15 mL) water.

4. Meanwhile, in the high-powered blender, add reserved onion, tofu, the remaining 1 tbsp (15 mL) olive oil, Dijon, nutritional yeast, garlic powder and turmeric; blend on high speed, adding soy milk in a steady stream through the hole in the lid. You may have to stop the motor to scrape down the sides of the blender. Add rice flour, cornstarch, bouillon, 1 tsp (5 mL) kala namak and ¼ tsp (1 mL) pepper; blend on high speed until smooth. The mixture should resemble pancake batter. If it's too thin, add 1 tbsp (15 mL) more rice flour. Season to taste with kala namak and pepper.

5. To tofu batter, stir in spinach mixture, tomatoes, dairy-free Parmesan, herbs de provence and nutmeg.

6. Spoon tofu mixture evenly into tart shells, using the back of a spoon to flatten the tops.

7. Place in the preheated oven and bake for 15 to 20 minutes, until the filling is set and pastry is browned.

8. Remove muffin tin from the oven and let cool on a wire rack for 5 minutes. Gently remove the quiches from the muffin tin and serve.

EGGS & THE CITY OMELET

SERVES 4

In my twenties, brunch was the only option available when you woke up late after a 4 a.m. night. But now that I'm in my thirties, it is an affair! I dress up, I wear a jaunty hat and I make these soft, loaded mushrooms and spinach omelets for my girlfriends. Host your next at-home brunch with a theme! My last one was rich widows. Dark, I know, but playing a game of "Did or didn't she kill him?" makes for great brunch entertainment.

• HIGH-POWERED BLENDER

OMELET BATTER

1 package (16 oz/450 g) soft tofu, drained

¾ cup (175 mL) dried yellow lentils, soaked overnight, drained and rinsed

3 tbsp (45 mL) nutritional yeast

1 cube (1 tsp/5 mL) vegetable bouillon

1 tsp (5 mL) garlic powder

1 tsp (5 mL) onion powder

1 tsp (5 mL) ground turmeric

Kala namak or sea salt

Freshly ground black pepper

FILLING

3 tbsp (45 mL) olive oil, divided

6 cups (1.5 L) cremini mushrooms, sliced

1 small onion, diced

4 garlic cloves, minced

6 cups (1.5 L) baby spinach

1 lemon wedge

Kala namak or sea salt

Freshly ground black pepper

1 cup (250 mL) dairy-free cheese of choice (optional)

1 tbsp (15 mL) chopped chives

1 **OMELET BATTER** In the high-powered blender, combine tofu, lentils, nutritional yeast, bouillon, garlic powder, onion powder, turmeric and 1 tsp (5 mL) kala namak; blend on high speed until smooth, stopping to scrape down the sides of the blender as needed. Taste and season with kala namak and pepper. Set aside.

2 **FILLING** In a large nonstick skillet, heat 2 tbsp (30 mL) olive oil over medium-high heat. Add mushrooms, onion and garlic; cook, stirring occasionally, for 3 to 5 minutes, until mushrooms are browned. Add spinach; cook, stirring occasionally, for 3 minutes, until wilted. Add a squeeze of lemon juice and season to taste with kala namak and pepper. Transfer mixture to a medium bowl and set aside. Wipe the skillet clean.

3 In the reserved skillet, heat 1 tsp (5 mL) olive oil over medium heat, swirling to coat the bottom. Working in batches, add ½ cup (125 mL) omelet batter and spread it out gently with a spatula. Cook for 2 to 3 minutes, until bubbles appear on the surface and the bottom is browning in spots.

4 Sprinkle ¼ cup (60 mL) dairy-free cheese (if using) and one-quarter of the filling on one side of the omelet; fold in half. Cook for 2 minutes, or until filling is warm and cheese begins to melt. Flip and cook for another 2 minutes, or until the bottom is lightly browned. Repeat with the remaining batter, dairy-free cheese and filling, adjusting heat and oiling the skillet between batches as necessary. Top with chives and serve as you go or keep warm in an oven preheated to 200°F (100°C) until ready to serve (and save the chive sprinkling for later).

Brunch in the
city has become a
multidisciplinary art.

FUL MEDAMES (AKA CREAMY EGYPTIAN BREAKFAST BEANS)

SERVES 4

Do you find yourself stuck in a cycle of dating the same trash human *(or different iterations of said human)*? If he's ignoring your texts and constantly canceling plans last minute, then, girl, cut him off. So, let's try putting something good and substantial into your body first thing in the morning for a change . . . like these perfectly seasoned tahini- and tomato-stewed Egyptian breakfast beans! Eat these slow-simmered favas right out of the pot, or set up a gorgeous, abundant, Arabic-style buffet. Because you *can* build a breakfast, but you can't build a boyfriend.

2 tbsp (30 mL) olive oil

1 small onion, diced

4 garlic cloves, crushed

2 tsp (10 mL) ground cumin

¼ tsp (1 mL) red pepper flakes

1 can (14 oz/398 mL) diced tomatoes (with juice)

1 can (14 oz/398 mL) fava beans (with liquid)

1 can (14 oz/398 mL) chickpeas, drained and rinsed

Sea salt and freshly ground black pepper

4 pitas

3 tbsp (45 mL) freshly squeezed lemon juice

2 tbsp (30 mL) tahini

Extra virgin olive oil

OPTIONAL ACCOMPANIMENTS

2 plum (Roma) tomatoes, diced

½ cup (125 mL) fresh parsley, chopped

1 small red onion, diced

Tahini

Red pepper flakes

Lemon wedges

1. In a medium saucepan, heat olive oil over medium-high heat. Add onion; cook, stirring occasionally, for 3 to 5 minutes, until translucent. Add garlic, cumin and red pepper flakes; cook for 1 minute, or until fragrant. Add tomatoes (with juice), fava beans (with liquid) and chickpeas, season to taste with sea salt and pepper, then bring to a boil. Reduce heat to medium, cover and simmer, stirring occasionally, for about 10 minutes, until beans are heated through and tender and the liquid has reduced by half.

2. Meanwhile, wrap pitas in damp paper towel. Microwave on High in 30-second intervals until warm. Remove from microwave and keep covered.

3. Remove the saucepan from the heat and stir in lemon juice and tahini.

4. Divide the ful among four shallow bowls, creating a divot in the center of each. Lightly drizzle extra virgin olive oil in divot. Place any accompaniment you are using in its own bowl with a spoon. Serve with pitas alongside. Let each person garnish their portion with the ingredients you laid out.

MAMA MICHAELA'S CAPPUCCINO YOGURT

SERVES 4 TO 6

I have this memory of my mom sitting on our balcony in Germany, eating cappuccino yogurt. She is visibly enjoying savoring each bite while telling us that we couldn't have any: "Eet has caf-e-eine, zerfore eet es for adults." In hoarding her dessert (and sometimes breakfast and snack), she taught me an important lesson — always use fear to keep others away from your favorite foods.

• HIGH-POWERED BLENDER

¼ **cup (60 mL)** boiling water

⅓ **cup (75 mL)** raw cashews

1 cup (250 mL) unsweetened soy milk

⅓ **cup (75 mL)** coconut cream

¼ **cup (60 mL)** pure maple syrup

¼ **tsp (1 mL)** vanilla extract

3 tbsp (45 mL) cornstarch

1 tbsp (15 mL) instant coffee granules

⅛ **tsp (0.5 mL)** sea salt

1   In the high-powered blender, combine boiling water and cashews; blend on high speed until smooth. Add soy milk, coconut cream, maple syrup, vanilla, cornstarch, instant coffee and sea salt; blend on high speed until smooth.

2   Transfer to a small saucepan and bring just to a boil, whisking constantly. Remove from heat.

3   Transfer to an uncovered airtight container to cool and thicken. Refrigerate until cold, 30 to 60 minutes depending on your fridge. I don't live with you, so do what feels right! (Once cold, cover and store for up to 5 days.)

4   Stir well before serving. Eat this heavenly yogurt on its own, with granola and berries or add to smoothies.

HACK IT!

Can't handle caffeine? Use instant decaf! It's just as tasty, without the jitters.

NINETIES KID FRENCH TOAST

SERVES 4

Ahhhh, the nineties. What a weird, fever-dreamlike time to be a kid. A decade where we ate sugary cereal, watched brain-melting Saturday morning cartoons, tried to keep our digital pocket pets alive, all while dressing like a Spice Girl and ASL-ing *(if you know, you know)* strangers on the internet. This recipe is an homage to that super confusing era — a mash-up of buttery, soft French toast wrapped in a crunchy caramel coating.

• HIGH-POWERED BLENDER
• GRIDDLE (OPTIONAL)

½ cup (125 mL) medium-firm tofu, pressed (page 15) and coarsely chopped

½ cup (125 mL) unsweetened soy milk

2 tbsp (30 mL) dairy-free butter, melted

½ tsp (2 mL) vanilla extract

2 tbsp (30 mL) nutritional yeast

½ tsp (2 mL) ground cinnamon

¼ tsp (1 mL) kala namak or sea salt

6 cups (1.5 L) Cap'n Crunch cereal, crushed (see *Hack It!*)

1 tbsp (15 mL) dairy-free butter (approx.)

8 thick sandwich bread slices

OPTIONAL TOPPINGS

Pure maple syrup

Confectioners' (icing) sugar

Fresh fruit

Dairy-free whipped topping

1   Preheat the oven to 200°F (100°C).

2   In the high-powered blender, combine tofu, soy milk, melted dairy-free butter, vanilla, nutritional yeast, cinnamon and kala namak; blend until smooth and creamy. Transfer to a medium shallow bowl. Place crushed cereal in a second shallow bowl.

3   Heat the 1 tbsp (15 mL) dairy-free butter in the griddle or a large skillet over medium heat. Working in batches (you should be able to fit at least 2 slices of bread in the skillet), dip a slice of bread into the tofu mixture and coat both sides generously, allowing any excess to drip off. Then place bread slice in the crushed cereal and press gently to coat; flip and repeat to coat the second side. Place in the skillet. Cook for 3 to 4 minutes on each side, until golden brown. Transfer to a baking sheet and place in the preheated oven to keep warm. Repeat with the remaining bread, tofu mixture and cereal, adjusting heat and buttering the skillet between batches as necessary.

4   Get creative with the toppings (if using) and serve. Or serve the French toast on a platter with the toppings in little bowls, and let everyone do their own thing.

HACK IT!

Try this recipe with Corn Flakes, Frosted Flakes, Froot Loops or, really, any sugary childhood cereal you love!

SON OF A BISCUIT! BANANA BREAD MUFFINS

MAKES 1 DOZEN MUFFINS

These muffins really take the biscuit and are perfect for when you just can't decide between bread, cupcakes and cookies. Think of them as a sneaky little treat you can pass off as a well-balanced meal.

- • ELECTRIC MIXER
- • 12-CUP MUFFIN TIN LINED WITH PAPER LINERS, AND TOP OF THE TIN GREASED

BISCOFF TOPPING

3 tbsp (45 mL) dairy-free butter or margarine, melted

½ cup (125 mL) crushed Biscoff cookies (see *Hack It!*)

2 tbsp (30 mL) unbleached all-purpose flour

2 tbsp (30 mL) brown sugar

¼ tsp (1 mL) ground cinnamon

MUFFINS

1½ tbsp (22 mL) ground flaxseed

¼ cup (60 mL) water

2¼ cups (560 mL) unbleached all-purpose flour

1½ tsp (7 mL) baking soda

¾ tsp (3 mL) baking powder

¾ tsp (3 mL) ground cinnamon

½ tsp (2 mL) sea salt

¼ tsp (1 mL) ground nutmeg

4 overripe bananas, mashed

¾ cup (175 mL) organic granulated sugar

⅓ cup (75 mL) dairy-free butter or margarine, softened

¼ cup (60 mL) unsweetened applesauce

¼ cup (60 mL) unsweetened soy milk

2 tsp (10 mL) vanilla extract

1 tsp (5 mL) apple cider vinegar

1 Preheat the oven to 425°F (220°C).

2 **BISCOFF TOPPING** In a small bowl, combine melted butter, crushed cookies, flour, brown sugar and cinnamon. Set aside.

3 **MUFFINS** In a separate small bowl, whisk together flaxseed and water. Set aside.

4 In a medium bowl, whisk together flour, baking soda, baking powder, cinnamon, sea salt and nutmeg. Set aside.

5 In the bowl of the stand mixer fitted with the paddle attachment (or in a large bowl using an electric hand mixer), beat flaxseed mixture, bananas, sugar, dairy-free butter, applesauce, soy milk, vanilla and apple cider vinegar to combine. Add flour mixture and beat to combine.

6 Spoon batter into the prepared muffin tin, filling the cups all the way to the top. Sprinkle the Biscoff topping evenly over each muffin.

7 Bake in the preheated oven for 5 minutes, then reduce oven temperature to 375°F (190°C) and bake for another 12 to 14 minutes, until a tester inserted into the center of a muffin comes out clean.

8 Remove muffins from the oven and let cool for 5 minutes in the muffin tin. Transfer to a wire rack to cool completely or eat one while they're warm!

HACK IT!

Biscoff cookies, also called speculoos, taste like a gingerbread-ish, dark caramel–flavored shortbread cookie. This Dutch staple is often served with tea or coffee and readily available at most grocery stores. (And Lotus brand is vegan!)

HACK IT!

Make these muffins gluten-free by swapping out the all-purpose flour for gluten-free flour (1:1) and top with your favorite gluten-free cookies.

UN-BE-
LEAF-
ABLE
SALADS

ˌən-bē-'lēv-ə-bəl \ ˈsa-ləds *(noun)*

1. **Unbelievable:** something so astounding or ridiculous it can't possibly be real. *"Man, I danced so hard! That DJ was unbelievable!"*

2. **Salad:** a dish containing a mélange of cold and sometimes warm ingredients, eaten either as a meal or with other food. *"Excuse me, do you think I can get my burger with half salad, half fries?"*

~~~~~~

Unbelievable salads are the *only* acceptable salad. What you won't find in this chapter is sad limp greens with a hint of olive oil. No, no, no — within these next few pages are salads of girth and means. Bold flavors and power-packed ingredients. Salads truly worthy of the word "meal."

KIMCHI CUTE-CUMBER SALAD

SERVES 4 TO 5

You know when you're making dinner and suddenly realize there isn't a single green thing on your plate? That's when I pull an ol' tried-and-true out of my back pocket. This kimchi cucumber salad is a nutritious addition to any meal, as well as a very effective hangover snack, one that sustained me during the summer of 2006, when I was a student, bartender and full-time party girl. It's a mind-tickling collision of fresh, spicy, sweet and sour that's cheap and easy and makes for good leftovers.

2 tbsp (30 mL) seasoned rice vinegar

2 tbsp (30 mL) toasted sesame oil

2 tsp (10 mL) chili garlic sauce

2 tsp (10 mL) pure maple syrup

2 English cucumbers, cut into half-moons or thinly sliced into ribbons

½ tsp (2 mL) sea salt

½ cup (125 mL) vegan-friendly kimchi

3 tbsp (45 mL) chopped fresh cilantro

2 tsp (10 mL) sesame seeds

1   In a large bowl, whisk together rice vinegar, sesame oil, chili garlic sauce and maple syrup.

2   Add cucumbers and toss to coat. Add sea salt and toss again. Add kimchi and cilantro; gently stir to combine. Sprinkle with sesame seeds. Serve immediately or store in an airtight container in the fridge for up to 3 days.

HACK IT!

Oh gosh! You've run out of kimchi! No problem, you can replace it with pickled items like pickles, onions or — and it's very German of me to suggest — sauerkraut. *Guten appetit!*

IMPASTA PESTO SALAD

SERVES 4

This is one of my favorite hot pastas . . . cosplaying as a salad. Literally, I took a comforting pesto pasta dish and made it cold with all the components of a salad. Think pesto vinaigrette, fresh uncooked veggies, greens and a tangy tofu feta. Diabolical? Or a stroke of genius?

• FOOD PROCESSOR

½ **cup (125 mL)** firm tofu, pressed (page 15) and crumbled

¼ **cup (60 mL)** sauerkraut brine or olive brine

1 **tsp (5 mL)** nutritional yeast

Sea salt

2 **cups (500 mL)** fusilli pasta

1 **cup (250 mL)** fresh basil

1 garlic clove

¼ **cup (60 mL)** extra virgin olive oil

2 **tbsp (30 mL)** red wine vinegar

1 **tbsp (15 mL)** freshly squeezed lemon juice

Freshly ground black pepper

1½ **cups (375 mL)** cooked cannellini (white kidney) beans, drained

1 yellow bell pepper, diced

1 **cup (250 mL)** packed spinach, chopped

½ small red onion, chopped

1. In a medium bowl, toss tofu with sauerkraut brine, nutritional yeast and ½ tsp (2 mL) sea salt to coat. Set aside.

2. Bring a large pot of salted water to a boil. Cook pasta according to package instructions. Drain pasta in a colander and set aside to cool.

3. Meanwhile, make a quick pesto vinaigrette in the food processor: combine basil, garlic, olive oil, red wine vinegar and lemon juice; pulse until finely chopped. Season with ¼ tsp (1 mL) sea salt and ¼ tsp (1 mL) pepper. Set aside.

4. In a large bowl, toss cooled pasta with pesto vinaigrette to coat. Add cannellini beans, yellow pepper, spinach, onion and tofu mixture; gently toss everything together. Season to taste with sea salt and pepper.

5. If you have time, let this salad sit in the fridge for at least 30 minutes or for up to 3 days to let the flavors meld. If you're pressed for time, serve right away.

PAPA'S POTATO SALAD

SERVES 4 TO 6

My dad picked up this recipe in the eighties while stationed in Germany with the army. The only thing keeping this salad from being every German stereotype is its lack of brats. Potatoes, check. Pickled something, check. Mustard, check. The flavor combo gets even better the more you let it sit, unlike your breath after eating a plate of this stuff.

2½ lbs (1.25 kg) Yukon gold potatoes, peeled and cut into 1-inch (2.5 cm) chunks

Sea salt

1 garlic clove, minced

¼ cup (60 mL) dill pickle juice

2 tbsp (30 mL) white wine vinegar

1 tbsp (15 mL) Dijon mustard

¼ cup (60 mL) olive oil

2 stalks celery, chopped

2 green onions, chopped

½ cup (125 mL) chopped white onion

½ cup (125 mL) dill pickles, chopped

¼ cup (60 mL) flat-leaf (Italian) parsley, finely chopped

1 tbsp (15 mL) dried dill

Freshly ground black pepper

1 Place potatoes in a large pot and add enough water to cover by 1 inch (2.5 cm). Add 1 tbsp (15 mL) sea salt and bring to a boil over high heat. Reduce heat to medium, cover and simmer for about 20 minutes, until potatoes are tender. Drain in a colander and let drip-dry completely.

2 Meanwhile, in a small bowl, whisk together garlic, pickle juice, white wine vinegar, Dijon and olive oil. Set aside.

3 In a large bowl, carefully combine cooked potatoes, celery, green onions, white onion, pickles, parsley and dill. Add pickle dressing to vegetables and stir gently to coat. Season to taste with sea salt and pepper.

4 Cover and chill in the fridge for at least 30 minutes or up to 5 days, or serve at room temperature (my personal favorite).

"THAT GIRL" BARLEY SALAD

SERVES 4 TO 6

You know that barley you bought because your fave #fitspo influencer told you it's totes healthy? But you cooked it once, decided it tasted like horse food and now it sits in the back of your pantry. This power salad is the perfect way to actually enjoy it! It has everything you see in those lunch bowls posted by "it girls." Packed with fresh veggies and crispy tofu smothered in a creamy tahini dressing, it will cost a fraction of what it does at *that* trendy lunch spot.

1 cup (250 mL) pearl barley

2 cups + 2 tbsp (530 mL) warm water (approx.), divided

1 garlic clove, minced

¾ tsp (3 mL) sea salt, divided

1 garlic clove, grated

⅓ cup (75 mL) tahini

2 tbsp (30 mL) freshly squeezed lemon juice (approx.)

1 tsp (5 mL) Dijon mustard

1 cup (250 mL) packed chopped arugula

4 green onions, thinly sliced

1 red bell pepper, diced

½ English cucumber, quartered lengthwise and sliced

1 ripe avocado, cubed

1 recipe Practically Perfect Crispy Tofu (page 180)

¼ cup (60 mL) chopped oil-packed sun-dried tomatoes

2 tbsp (30 mL) hemp hearts

1. In a medium saucepan, bring barley, 2 cups (500 mL) water, minced garlic and ¼ tsp (1 mL) sea salt to a boil over high heat. Reduce heat to medium-low, cover and simmer for about 30 minutes, until barley is tender and all the water has been absorbed. Transfer to the fridge to cool while you prepare the rest of the recipe.

2. In a small bowl, whisk together grated garlic, tahini, lemon juice, the remaining 2 tbsp (30 mL) warm water, Dijon and the remaining ½ tsp (2 mL) sea salt. The dressing should be smooth and pourable, so add an additional 1 tbsp (15 mL) water at a time, whisking in between additions, if necessary.

3. In a large serving bowl, combine cooked barley, arugula and green onions. Add red pepper, cucumber, avocado and tahini dressing; toss to combine. Top with tofu cubes, sun-dried tomatoes and hemp hearts. Serve as a meal or as a side. Leftovers will keep in an airtight container in the fridge for up to 3 days.

HACK IT!

Meal prep this salad for the week by evenly dividing the barley, arugula and green onions among four to six airtight containers; stir. In sections, arrange red pepper, cucumber and tofu cubes. Top with sun-dried tomatoes and hemp hearts. Add avocado and dressing just before serving.

AH, FREAK OUT! LE FREAK, C'EST GREEK!

SERVES 4

I have a confession: I don't like quinoa. *Gasp* I know, I know — I've committed an epic vegan sin. I've tried! Really, I did! I baked it, stuffed it, souped it, made it into patties and I just can't get over the birdseed aftertaste. One day, I had a leftover pile of it in my fridge from one of my experiments, and in one last-ditch effort, I tossed some into a Greek salad and it was ambrosian! Le freak! C'est chic!

½ cup (125 mL) firm tofu, pressed (page 15) and crumbled

¼ cup (60 mL) sauerkraut brine or olive brine

2 tsp (10 mL) nutritional yeast

Sea salt

1 cup (250 mL) quinoa, rinsed

2 cups (500 mL) water

¼ tsp (1 mL) freshly ground black pepper

2 garlic cloves, minced

1 tbsp (15 mL) fresh dill or 1 tsp (5 mL) dried dill

½ tsp (2 mL) dried oregano

3 tbsp (45 mL) freshly squeezed lemon juice

2 tbsp (30 mL) red wine vinegar

2 tbsp (30 mL) extra virgin olive oil

1 green bell pepper, diced

1 small red onion, minced

¼ English cucumber, halved lengthwise and quartered

1 cup (250 mL) cherry tomatoes, halved

½ cup (125 mL) pitted kalamata olives

½ cup (125 mL) chopped flat-leaf (Italian) parsley

1   In a medium bowl, toss tofu with sauerkraut brine, nutritional yeast and ¼ tsp (1 mL) sea salt to coat. Set aside to marinate.

2   In a medium saucepan, combine quinoa, water, ½ tsp (2 mL) sea salt and pepper; bring to a boil over high heat. Cover, then reduce heat to medium and simmer for 15 minutes, or until the water has been absorbed. Remove from heat, cover and let stand for 10 minutes. Fluff with a fork.

3   Meanwhile, in a large bowl, whisk together garlic, dill, oregano, lemon juice, red wine vinegar and olive oil.

4   To the large bowl, add marinated tofu, green pepper, red onion, cucumber, tomatoes, olives and parsley; toss with the dressing to coat. Cover and place in the fridge to chill for a minimum of 30 minutes or up to 5 days.

HACK IT!

This salad gets better the longer it stands. I actually love it even more the next day! Gotta love ambitious leftovers.

IT'S JUST A GRILLED CAESAR! ROMAINE CALM!

SERVES 4

Okay, so grilled lettuce is exactly what you would expect a vegan to bring to a BBQ. It sounds like living in a bad vegan joke, but I promise this eccentric salad is hands down the best salad you will ever make. After they taste the hot, browned and crispy ruffled edges, topped with tangy Caesar dressing and perfectly marinated tofu, the only thing they'll be laughing at is raw lettuce.

• BBQ OR 2 LARGE SKILLETS

½ cup (125 mL) soy sauce (see *Hack It!*)

⅓ cup (75 mL) apple cider vinegar or white wine vinegar

3 tbsp (45 mL) water

1 package (16 oz/450 g) firm tofu, pressed (page 15) and cut into 4-inch (10 cm) triangles

1 garlic clove, minced

2 tbsp (30 mL) olive oil (approx.), divided

1 tbsp (15 mL) freshly squeezed lemon juice

1 tbsp (15 mL) minced capers

1 tsp (5 mL) Dijon mustard

1 can (14 oz/398 mL) white beans, such as cannellini, drained and rinsed

Sea salt and freshly ground black pepper

¼ cup (60 mL) flat-leaf (Italian) parsley, chopped and divided

2 romaine lettuce heads, halved lengthwise, rinsed and patted dry

1 cup (250 mL) prepared vegan Caesar dressing

2 tbsp (30 mL) simulated bacon bits

2 tbsp (30 mL) whole capers

1 cup (250 mL) prepared hummus (optional but recommended)

1. In a medium shallow bowl, whisk together soy sauce, apple cider vinegar and water. Add tofu, turn to coat and set aside.

2. In a separate medium bowl, whisk together garlic, 1 tbsp (15 mL) olive oil, lemon juice, minced capers and Dijon.

3. Add white beans; gently toss to coat. Season to taste with sea salt and pepper. Add 2 tbsp (30 mL) parsley; toss to combine. Set aside.

4. **IF USING A BBQ** Preheat the BBQ to medium. Place marinated tofu on the BBQ grill (reserving marinade) and grill for 3 to 5 minutes on each side, until there are nice char marks, brushing with the extra marinade as needed to keep moist. Meanwhile, drizzle the remaining 1 tbsp (15 mL) olive oil over romaine halves and sprinkle with salt and pepper. Place on the grill, cut side down. Grill romaine for 2 to 3 minutes, until you have some nice char marks on the bottom. Flip and grill for another 1 to 2 minutes, until charred on the other side.

   IF USING A STOVETOP Heat 1 tbsp (15 mL) olive oil in a large skillet over medium-high heat. Fry tofu for 3 to 5 minutes on each side, until browned. Meanwhile, drizzle the remaining 1 tbsp (15 mL) olive oil over romaine heads and sprinkle with salt and pepper. Heat a separate large skillet over high heat. Working in batches, place romaine in the clean skillet, cut side down. Cook for 3 to 4 minutes, until browned. Flip, then cook for another 1 to 2 minutes, until browned on the other side.

HACK IT!

To make this recipe gluten-free, use tamari instead of soy sauce.

THREE WAYS

5 There are a few ways you can serve this salad:

A. Place romaine halves on a large serving platter. Top with bean mixture and tofu. Drizzle with Caesar dressing, then garnish with simulated bacon bits, whole capers and the remaining 2 tbsp (30 mL) parsley. I love to present it, then slice the romaine in front of my guests, allowing everyone to serve themselves their ideal piece. Serve with hummus on the side (if using).

B. Chop the romaine and add it to a salad bowl along with the bean mixture, simulated bacon bits, whole capers and the remaining 2 tbsp (30 mL) parsley. Drizzle with Caesar dressing and toss to mix. Top with tofu and serve with hummus on the side (if using).

C. Serve everyone their individual half of grilled romaine, topped with the bean mixture, a few pieces of tofu and a dollop of hummus (if using). Drizzle with Caesar dressing, and garnish with simulated bacon bits, whole capers and the remaining 2 tbsp (30 mL) parsley.

PEANUT BUTTER & JEALOUS NOODLE SALAD

SERVES 4 TO 6

It takes a lot to convince me that any salad can be (1) a meal and (2) satisfying. Some tomato-topped, limp-leafed, balsamic-coated pile of disappointment just won't cut it at Casa de Candice. Give me substance, give me texture and, perhaps most importantly, give me peanut butter.

• BLENDER

DRESSING

1 garlic clove, smashed

1 tbsp (15 mL) minced ginger

3 tbsp (45 mL) creamy peanut butter

2 tbsp (30 mL) tamari

2 tbsp (30 mL) seasoned rice vinegar

2 tbsp (30 mL) toasted sesame oil

2 tbsp (30 mL) freshly squeezed lime juice

1 tbsp (15 mL) pure maple syrup

½ to 1 tsp (2 to 5 mL) red pepper flakes

SALAD

Sea salt

8 oz (250 g) wide rice noodles

3 green onions, thinly sliced diagonally

2 carrots, peeled and sliced into ribbons (see *Hack It!*)

1 red bell pepper, diced

½ English cucumber, halved lengthwise and sliced

1 cup (250 mL) green cabbage, shredded

½ cup + 1 tbsp (140 mL) fresh cilantro, chopped and divided

½ tsp (2 mL) red pepper flakes (approx.) (optional)

Sea salt and freshly ground black pepper

1 tbsp (15 mL) sesame seeds

1 **DRESSING** In the blender, combine garlic, ginger, peanut butter, tamari, rice vinegar, sesame oil, lime juice and maple syrup; blend on high speed until smooth. Stir in red pepper flakes. Set aside.

2 **SALAD** Bring a large pot of salted water to a boil. Break rice noodles in half and add them to the pot; cook according to package instructions.

3 Drain noodles in a colander and place under cold water to stop them from cooking. Let drip-dry.

4 In a large bowl, combine green onions, carrots, red pepper, cucumber, cabbage, ½ cup (125 mL) cilantro and one-quarter of the dressing. Add rice noodles, drizzle with the remaining dressing and toss to combine.

5 Sprinkle with red pepper flakes, if desired, and season to taste with sea salt and pepper. Garnish with the remaining 1 tbsp (15 mL) cilantro and sesame seeds.

HACK IT!

To make carrots ribbons, using a vegetable peeler, peel along the length of the carrot from top to bottom. Now you have a ribbon! Rotate the carrot slightly and repeat until almost no carrot remains.

If you love heat, I highly recommend adding a chopped red Thai chili or two to this salad in Step 4. It is absolute perfection, but very spicy!

This salad is for those days when you need your noodle fix but it's too hot for ramen. Plus, the epic leftovers make this the ultimate dinner-to-desk-lunch that doubles as a summer picnic star.

NO-FAIL KALE MISO SLAW

SERVES 4 TO 6

Need a kale salad for someone who hates kale? This is *that* salad. The key is to let this vinegar-and-miso-drenched pile of magic sit for as long as possible. Like a fine wine, the kale only gets better with age but, of course, eating it right away is also delish. Oh, and if you find yourself drinking this tangy dressing straight, I won't judge you.

APPLE CIDER–MISO DRESSING

2 tbsp (30 mL) apple cider vinegar

2 tbsp (30 mL) white or yellow miso paste

2 tbsp (30 mL) extra virgin olive oil

1½ tsp (7 mL) pure maple syrup

1½ tsp (7 mL) water

SALAD

8 cups (2 L) finely shredded dinosaur kale (about 1 bunch)

1 red bell pepper, chopped into bite-sized pieces

2 cups (500 mL) shredded carrots

½ cup (125 mL) thinly sliced red onion

⅓ cup (75 mL) hemp hearts

1 **APPLE CIDER–MISO DRESSING** In a medium bowl, whisk together apple cider vinegar, miso paste, olive oil, maple syrup and water. Set aside.

2 **SALAD** In a large bowl, toss kale with one-third of the dressing. Massage kale with your hands until wilted. Add red pepper, carrots, onion and another one-third of the dressing; toss to coat. Add more dressing as desired to taste. (I love a lot of dressing, but you may not!) Add hemp hearts and toss to mix.

3 Serve immediately or store in the fridge in an airtight container for up to 5 days.

CRISPY CHOPPED SALAD

SERVES 4

It's not, like, a regular salad; it's a cool salad. Well, technically it's a cool salad topped with warm chickpeas. Think of it as a superior version of a traditional chopped salad, only with heartier veggies and a classic herb vinaigrette.

⅓ **cup (75 mL)** extra virgin olive oil, divided

1 can (14 oz/398 mL) chickpeas, drained, rinsed and patted dry

1 tbsp (15 mL) nutritional yeast

1 tsp (5 mL) dried parsley

1 tsp (5 mL) dried dill

½ **tsp (2 mL)** garlic powder

½ **tsp (2 mL)** onion powder

Sea salt and freshly ground black pepper

1 garlic clove, grated

1 tbsp (15 mL) chopped fresh parsley

½ **tsp (2 mL)** dried basil

3 tbsp (45 mL) white wine vinegar

2 cups (500 mL) packed chopped spinach

1 pint (12 oz/340 g) cherry tomatoes, halved

½ English cucumber, sliced into thin half-moons

½ **cup (125 mL)** Mixed Herb & Garlic Chèvre (page 111) or dairy-free chèvre, crumbled

1   In a medium skillet, heat 2 tbsp (30 mL) olive oil over medium heat. Add chickpeas, nutritional yeast, dried parsley, dill, garlic powder, onion powder, ½ tsp (2 mL) sea salt and ¼ tsp (1 mL) pepper. Cook, stirring frequently, for 10 to 15 minutes, until chickpeas are golden and crispy. Set aside.

2   Meanwhile, in a salad bowl, whisk together garlic, fresh parsley, basil, white wine vinegar and the remaining 3 tbsp (45 mL) olive oil. Season to taste with sea salt and pepper. Add spinach, tomatoes and cucumber; toss to mix. Scatter crispy chickpeas and chèvre overtop; serve.

HACK IT!

Try this classic herb vinaigrette on other salads you like to make. It will always be delicious and is a great recipe to know by heart.

BROC 'N' SLAW

SERVES 4

Once upon a time, I worked in the corporate world *(shudder)*. The only thing I liked at work, besides the coffee, was this salad. It's easy to make ahead, inexpensive and full of fresh ingredients that are tossed in a creamy dill dressing — keeping your lunch game strong through the entire week. Or try it alongside my Gooey Messy Lentil Burger aka Sloppy Joe (page 147).

½ **cup (125 mL)** plain coconut yogurt

½ **cup (125 mL)** egg-free mayo

2 **tbsp (30 mL)** minced capers

2 **tbsp (30 mL)** white wine vinegar

2 **tbsp (30 mL)** chopped fresh dill or 2 tsp (10 mL) dried dill

1 **tsp (5 mL)** garlic powder

Sea salt

1 green apple, cut into matchsticks

½ **can (14 oz/398 mL)** butter beans or lima beans, drained and rinsed

½ small red onion, finely chopped

1 **lb (500 g)** broccoli, shredded (see *Hack It!*)

¼ **cup (60 mL)** chopped fresh parsley

¼ **cup (60 mL)** sunflower seeds

1 In a large bowl, whisk together coconut yogurt, egg-free mayo, capers, white wine vinegar, dill and garlic powder to combine. Season to taste with sea salt.

2 To the bowl, add apple, butter beans, onion, broccoli and parsley; toss to coat. Season to taste with sea salt.

3 Sprinkle with sunflower seeds and serve immediately or store in an airtight container in the fridge for up to 5 days.

HACK IT!

Shred broccoli using a box grater (don't forget the stems!) or put it in your food processor and process into shreds.

You can also use this dressing as a veggie dip. You'll never go back to ranch again!

NEW YORK DELI MAC SALAD

SERVES 4

I'm not going to try to sell you on macaroni salad. It's iconic. Heck, if I could sing even a little bit, I would write a John Mayer–esque love song about it. I love pasta salad any way you want to give it to me, but a deli-style mac salad is in a field of its own. I keep it traditional with a tart-but-sweet mayo dressing, red pepper and red onion, because this is a classic you just don't mess with.

2½ cups (625 mL) macaroni

1 cup (250 mL) egg-free mayo

3 tbsp (45 mL) apple juice

3 tbsp (45 mL) apple cider vinegar

1 tsp (5 mL) yellow mustard

Sea salt and freshly ground black pepper

2 stalks celery, diced

1 red pepper, diced

¼ small red onion, diced

¼ cup (60 mL) fresh parsley, chopped

1 Bring a large pot of salted water to a boil. Add pasta and cook according to package instructions. Drain pasta in a colander (reserving pot). Set aside to cool.

2 Meanwhile, in a small bowl, whisk together egg-free mayo, apple juice, apple cider vinegar and yellow mustard. Season to taste with sea salt and pepper.

3 Once macaroni has cooled, return it to the pot along with the celery, red pepper, onion, parsley and dressing; toss to coat. Season to taste with sea salt and pepper, cover and refrigerate for a minimum of 30 minutes or up to 5 days.

HACK IT!

This is another it-gets-better-with-age salad, making it an awesome make-ahead recipe.

oy!

SOUP

keep your fingers

DU

out of my soup!

JOUR

ˌsüp \ də \ ˈzhu̇r *(noun)*

1. A delicious liquid made by combining simmering vegetables and various ingredients, featured on a particular day. *"Excuse me, Flo, what's the soup du jour?"*

2. A tried-and-true remedy for everything from a hangover to the flu. *"If you're feeling like poo, a soup will do!"*

Like a little black dress, (the often underrated) soup is an essential. It is an obvious choice for a quick and easy after-work dinner but also serves as a fail-safe for those weeks (*yes, weeks*) when you've got nothing but prosecco in the fridge and a nearly empty cupboard. It's notoriously hard to mess up making soup, so even on your most inept of days, you can pull off something scrumptious.

THIS SOUP IS SPEC-TACO-LAR

SERVES 4 TO 6

If a taco dressed up as a soup for Halloween, you'd end up with this recipe. It's a soul-soothing, tongue-enticing bowl of goodness that eats like a meal. Think of it like a liquid taco, sprinkled with all your fave Tex-Mex toppings. Throw on some music and you've got yourself a fiesta in the kitchen *and* in your belly.

1 tbsp (15 mL) coconut oil

1 small onion, diced

2 garlic cloves, minced

1½ tsp (7 mL) seeded and chopped jalapeño pepper (optional)

Sea salt

1 can (28 oz/796 mL) diced tomatoes (with juice)

1 can (14 oz/398 mL) black beans (with liquid)

1 can (14 oz/398 mL) kidney beans (with liquid)

2 cups (500 mL) frozen corn

1 package (1 oz/30 g) taco seasoning

2 cubes (each 1 tsp/5 mL) no-beef or vegetable bouillon

4 cups (1 L) water

Freshly ground black pepper

OPTIONAL TOPPINGS

Crushed tortilla chips (see *Hack It!*)

Sliced green onion

Sliced avocado

Dairy-free sour cream

Dairy-free Cheddar cheese or mozzarella cheese shreds

Chopped fresh cilantro

1 In a large pot, heat coconut oil over medium heat. Add onion; cook, stirring occasionally, for 3 to 5 minutes, until translucent. Add garlic, jalapeño (if using) and ½ tsp (2 mL) sea salt; cook, stirring constantly, for 2 to 3 minutes, until garlic is fragrant.

2 Add tomatoes (with juice), black beans and kidney beans (with their liquid), corn, taco seasoning, bouillon and water; stir and bring to a boil over high heat. Reduce heat to medium and simmer for 20 minutes, stirring occasionally, or until flavors have melded.

3 Season to taste with sea salt and pepper. Ladle soup into bowls and garnish with toppings (if using).

HACK IT!

Most tortilla chips are made with corn and therefore gluten-free, but make sure to check the ingredients if you're avoiding gluten to ensure they do not include wheat.

CHEAP & CHEERFUL RAMEN-STYLE SOUP

SERVES 4

This soup isn't by-the-book ramen, so it would be wrong to call it that. But it is inspired by ramen, and absolutely scratches that itch. It's for those of us who save our take-out money for wine and who triple-steep our tea bags. A quick blender broth and instant noodles make this a lazy dupe for the near-sacred soup.

• BAKING SHEET LINED WITH PARCHMENT PAPER
• BLENDER

CRISPY TOFU

¼ cup (60 mL) soy sauce, divided

2 tsp (10 mL) cornstarch

1 package (16 oz/450 g) extra-firm tofu, pressed (page 15) and cubed

BROTH

4 packages (each 5 oz/150 g) dried ramen noodles

2 tbsp (30 mL) toasted sesame oil

1 small onion, chopped

4 garlic cloves, minced

8 cups (2 L) vegetable broth

2 tbsp (30 mL) nutritional yeast

1 tbsp (15 mL) minced ginger

1 tbsp (15 mL) tahini

1 tbsp (15 mL) mirin

3 tbsp (45 mL) white miso paste

FIXINGS

2 tbsp (30 mL) toasted sesame oil

4 cups (1 L) sliced mushrooms

4 cups (1 L) shredded green cabbage

1 cup (250 mL) corn

½ cup (125 mL) green onions, chopped

¼ tsp (1 mL) red pepper flakes

I Put That Sh*t on Everything Chili Oil (page 196) or chili oil

1 tsp (5 mL) sesame seeds

1. **CRISPY TOFU** Preheat the oven to 400°F (200°C).

2. In a medium bowl, whisk together 3 tbsp (45 mL) soy sauce and cornstarch. Add tofu cubes and toss to coat.

3. Arrange tofu in a single layer on the prepared baking sheet, spacing ½ inch (1 cm) apart. Bake in the preheated oven for 15 minutes, flipping halfway, or until golden brown.

4. **BROTH** Meanwhile, bring a large pot of water to a boil. Add ramen noodles and cook according to package instructions. Drain (reserving pot) and divide noodles among four bowls. Set aside.

5. Meanwhile, heat sesame oil in the reserved pot over medium heat. Add onion and garlic; cook, stirring occasionally, for 3 to 5 minutes, until onion is translucent. Transfer onion mixture to the blender (reserving pot).

6. To the blender, add broth, nutritional yeast, ginger, the remaining 1 tbsp (15 mL) soy sauce, tahini and mirin; blend on high speed until smooth.

7. Transfer broth mixture to the reserved pot and bring to a boil over high heat. Reduce heat to medium and simmer for about 15 minutes, until flavors have melded. Transfer 1 cup (250 mL) broth from the saucepan to a small bowl and whisk in miso until dissolved. Pour mixture into the saucepan and stir to combine. Keep warm over low heat.

8. **FIXINGS** Meanwhile, in a large skillet, heat sesame oil over high heat. Add mushrooms and cook for 3 to 5 minutes, until slightly browned. Reduce heat to medium-high; add cabbage, corn, green onions and red pepper flakes; cook for 3 to 5 minutes, until heated through. Set aside.

9. Ladle broth into the noodle bowls. I like about 2 cups (500 mL) per person. Top with sautéed veggies and crispy tofu, and garnish with chili oil and sesame seeds.

GOOFPROOF MINESTRONE

SERVES 4 TO 6

Did you just spend an entire hour bragging about your mad kitchen "skills" to impress a date, when, in actuality, your real idea of cooking entails hitting the Defrost button on your microwave? Did they fall for it and now want to come over for dinner? I got you, ya silly goof! This minestrone is "your mother's recipe." This robust and hearty one-pot dish passes as a full meal, but it's easy enough for even *you* to throw together.

2 tbsp (30 mL) olive oil

2 large carrots, halved lengthwise and sliced

2 stalks celery, chopped

1 small onion, chopped

3 garlic cloves, minced

Sea salt

1 tbsp (15 mL) dried basil

1 tsp (5 mL) dried parsley

1 tsp (5 mL) dried oregano

½ tsp (2 mL) dried thyme

1 bay leaf

1½ cubes (each 1 tsp/5 mL) no-beef or vegetable bouillon

2 tbsp (30 mL) nutritional yeast (approx.)

1 can (28 oz/796 mL) diced tomatoes (with juice)

1 can (14 oz/398 mL) kidney beans, drained and rinsed

1 can (14 oz/398 mL) white beans, such as cannellini, drained and rinsed

6 cups (1.5 L) water

¼ cup (60 mL) tomato paste

1 cup (250 mL) elbow or penne pasta

2 cups (500 mL) packed baby spinach, chopped kale or chopped collard greens

Freshly ground black pepper (optional)

1 In a large pot, heat olive oil over medium-high heat. Add carrots, celery, onion, garlic and a pinch of sea salt; cook, stirring constantly, for 5 to 7 minutes, until tender. Stir in basil, parsley, oregano, thyme and bay leaf.

2 Add bouillon cubes, yeast, tomatoes (with juice), kidney beans, white beans, water and tomato paste; stir to combine. Bring to a boil. Reduce heat to medium-low and simmer for 10 minutes, or until flavors have melded. Add pasta, cover with a lid and cook for another 10 minutes, or until pasta is tender and the soup has thickened slightly.

3 Stir in baby spinach and cook for about 3 minutes, until wilted. Season to taste with sea salt.

4 Divide soup among bowls. Sprinkle with nutritional yeast to finish, and add some freshly ground black pepper from a giant peppermill if you really wanna show off. I recommend serving with some crusty bread on the side, but, like, live your life how *you* want.

HACK IT!

Cook your favorite plant-based sausage according to the package instructions in the pot before the veggies in Step 1, remove it and then add it back in Step 3. Tasty!

HIGHER MORELS CREAMY MUSHROOM SOUP

SERVES 4

While this recipe does not, in fact, contain morels, holy shiitake is this the soup for you mushroom lovers out there! The magic is in its simplicity. It's easy enough to whip up in a flash, but fancy, thick and rich enough to serve if you're entertaining a fun guy for dinner.

• BLENDER

¼ cup (60 mL) olive oil

2 lbs (1 kg) cremini mushrooms, chopped

1 small onion, chopped

Sea salt

4 garlic cloves, minced

⅓ cup (75 mL) unbleached all-purpose flour

Water

3 cubes (each 1 tsp/5 mL) no-beef or vegetable bouillon

1 bay leaf

1 tsp (5 mL) dried thyme

Freshly ground black pepper

1   In a large pot, heat olive oil over medium-high heat. Add mushrooms, onion and ½ tsp (2 mL) sea salt; cook, stirring occasionally, for 3 to 5 minutes, until mushrooms have released their liquid. Reduce heat to medium and add garlic; cook, stirring often, for about 15 minutes, until mushrooms are swimming in their own liquid.

2   Add flour and toss to coat mushrooms. Cook, stirring constantly, for 3 minutes, or until flour turns dark beige. Do not allow the flour to brown. If it becomes too dry, add 1 tbsp (15 mL) water at a time, until a paste forms.

3   Stir in bouillon, bay leaf, thyme and 8 cups (2 L) water; bring to a boil over high heat. Reduce heat to medium-low, partially cover, and simmer for 15 to 20 minutes, until thickened slightly.

4   Remove bay leaf and let soup cool slightly. Working in batches as necessary, transfer soup to the blender. Remove the plug in the lid and blend on high speed until smooth.

5   Return the blended soup to the pot and give it a good stir. Heat over medium until warmed.

6   Season to taste with sea salt and pepper; serve.

HACK IT!

Make this recipe gluten-free by substituting cornstarch for the flour.

GRATIFYING OKRA GUMBO

SERVES 4 TO 6

Some days I look up from my computer at 11:30 p.m. and realize that the only thing I have ingested that day is coffee! That's where this thick stew featuring plant-based sausage, okra and Cajun seasonings comes in. Gumbo is to Louisiana what chili is to Texas: a culinary staple that varies from cook to cook. I make a big batch of this on Sunday and heat it up during the week in less time than it takes to order takeout.

1 can (20 oz/590 g) young jackfruit in water or brine, drained and rinsed

1½ tsp (7 mL) paprika

1 tsp (5 mL) garlic powder

¼ tsp (1 mL) mustard powder

¼ tsp (1 mL) cayenne pepper

Freshly ground black pepper

7 tbsp (105 mL) dairy-free butter or margarine, divided

2 plant-based sausages (I like something spicy), cut into ¾-inch (2 cm) slices

⅓ cup (75 mL) unbleached all-purpose flour

2 stalks celery, chopped

1 small onion, chopped

½ green bell pepper, chopped

2 tbsp (30 mL) Cajun seasoning

Sea salt

2 cups (500 mL) sliced frozen or fresh okra

1¾ cups (425 mL) crushed tomatoes (with juice)

2 cubes (each 1 tsp/5 mL) no-chicken or vegetable bouillon

1 bay leaf

4 cups (1 L) water (approx.)

¼ cup (60 mL) fresh parsley, chopped

4 cups (1 L) cooked long-grain white or brown rice, warm

2 green onions, chopped

1. In a medium bowl, using a potato masher or fork, shred jackfruit. Add paprika, garlic powder, mustard powder, cayenne pepper and ¼ tsp (1 mL) pepper. Toss to coat jackfruit completely and set aside.

2. In a large pot, heat 1 tbsp (15 mL) dairy-free butter over medium-high heat. Add plant-based sausage and cook for 3 minutes, or until browned. Transfer to a large bowl (reserving pot).

3. Heat 2 tbsp (30 mL) dairy-free butter in the reserved pot over medium-high heat and add the spiced jackfruit; cook for 3 minutes, or until tender. Transfer jackfruit to the bowl with the plant-based sausage and set aside.

4. Reduce heat to medium and melt the remaining ¼ cup (60 mL) dairy-free butter. Add flour; cook, stirring constantly, for 10 minutes, until it turns dark brown.

5. Add celery, onion, green pepper, Cajun seasoning and ¼ tsp (1 mL) sea salt; cook, stirring occasionally, for about 3 minutes, until veggies are soft. Return the cooked sausage and jackfruit to the pot along with okra, tomatoes (with juice), bouillon, bay leaf and water; bring to a boil. Reduce heat to medium-low and simmer for 15 minutes or up to 1 hour depending on how much time you want to spend on dinner tonight. If your gumbo is thickening too quickly, add a touch more water to the pot. It should have the consistency of a chili.

6. Remove bay leaf and season to taste with sea salt and pepper. Stir in parsley and serve over cooked rice, garnished with green onions.

HACK IT!

There are so many delicious ways to serve this recipe: try it over roasted potatoes or with a side of cornbread or coleslaw — the contrasting flavors is near-perfection.

Jackfruit can sizes vary. I use the standard size of 20 oz (590 g), which gives me 10 oz (300 g) jackfruit once drained — the amount needed for this recipe!

CHICKPEA NOODLE SOUP

SERVES 4

Unlike the chicken noodle soup your mom whipped up when you were sick, this one is so easy that even the dude you've got kickin' around can't mess it up. It'll leave you not only nourished but rested and on the right track to feeling like your hot little self. Although not too hot — that's a fever. Edgy Veg tip: if you've got a head cold, add some hot sauce and watch those sinuses clear up in a flash!

2 tbsp (30 mL) olive oil

2 carrots, sliced

2 stalks celery, chopped

1 small onion, chopped

4 garlic cloves, minced

Sea salt

¼ cup (60 mL) nutritional yeast

1 tsp (5 mL) dried parsley

1 tsp (5 mL) dried basil

1 tsp (5 mL) dried oregano

Freshly ground black pepper

1 can (14 oz/398 mL) chickpeas, drained and rinsed

4 cubes (each 1 tsp/5 mL) no-chicken or vegetable bouillon

5 cups (1.25 L) water

2 cups (500 mL) rotini pasta

2 cups (500 mL) loosely packed baby spinach, coarsely chopped

¼ cup (60 mL) flat-leaf (Italian) parsley, chopped

Red pepper flakes (optional)

1 In a large pot, heat olive oil over medium-high heat. Add carrots, celery, onion, garlic and a pinch of sea salt; cook, stirring occasionally, for 3 to 5 minutes, until onion is translucent and vegetables are tender. Stir in nutritional yeast, dried parsley, basil, oregano and ¼ tsp (1 mL) pepper; cook for 2 minutes, or until fragrant.

2 Add chickpeas, bouillon and water; stir and bring to a boil. Reduce heat to medium, cover and simmer for 15 minutes, or until flavors have melded.

3 Stir in rotini and simmer for another 10 minutes, or until pasta is fork-tender.

4 Stir in spinach and fresh parsley; season to taste with sea salt and pepper. Cook for about 3 minutes, stirring occasionally, until spinach has wilted. Serve soup on its own or with a sprinkle of red pepper flakes (if using), a side of buttered toast and a box of tissues.

HACK IT!

Want to make this soup a bit heartier? Add 2 cups (500 mL) prepared chicken substitute or soy curls in Step 3.

A-MAIZE-ING CORN CHOWDER!

SERVES 4

Hey you! You look a little hungry. Would you like some soup? I made it myself. It's a warm, hearty, cling-to-your-ribs corn bath packed with veggies and made with love. *Sigh* I really do adore soups; nothing comforts me more. Easily make this recipe gluten-free by replacing the flour with cornstarch.

¼ **cup (60 mL)** olive oil, divided

3 large yellow potatoes, peeled and diced

2 stalks celery, chopped

2 large carrots, chopped

1 large onion, diced

3 garlic cloves, minced

Sea salt and freshly ground black pepper

¼ **cup (60 mL)** unbleached all-purpose flour

½ **cup (125 mL)** dry white wine

2 cups (500 mL) frozen corn kernels

¼ **cup (60 mL)** nutritional yeast

½ **tsp (2 mL)** dried thyme

½ **tsp (2 mL)** paprika

¼ **tsp (1 mL)** cayenne pepper

1 bay leaf

1 cube (1 tsp/5 mL) vegetable bouillon

5 cups (1.25 L) water

1 cup (250 mL) unsweetened soy milk

¼ **cup (60 mL)** chopped fresh parsley

1. In a large pot, heat 3 tbsp (45 mL) olive oil over medium-high heat. Add potatoes, celery, carrots, onion and garlic; cook, stirring constantly, for 3 to 5 minutes, until onion is translucent. Season with ½ tsp (2 mL) sea salt and ½ tsp (2 mL) pepper.

2. Add the remaining 1 tbsp (15 mL) olive oil and stir to coat the veggies. Add flour; stir to coat. Cook, stirring constantly, for 2 minutes, or until the flour forms a thick paste. Stir in white wine, making sure to scrape up any golden bits stuck to the bottom of the pot.

3. Add corn, nutritional yeast, thyme, paprika, cayenne pepper, bay leaf, bouillon and water; bring to a boil. Reduce heat to medium-low, cover and simmer for 15 minutes, or until potatoes are fork-tender.

4. Add soy milk and return to a boil. Reduce heat to medium-low and simmer for 3 to 5 minutes, until soup thickens slightly. Season to taste with sea salt and pepper. Remove bay leaf.

5. Garnish with parsley and serve with toasted bread.

HACK IT!

For a creamier soup, remove one-quarter of the soup at the end of Step 3, blend until smooth and then return it to the pot.

Try 1 cup (250 mL) of your favorite dairy-free shredded cheese and ¾ cup (175 mL) sliced cooked plant-based sausage mixed in at the end of Step 4. It's like a warm hug on a winter's day.

CLASSIC CHEESY CHILI

SERVES 4 TO 6

Most of us nineties kids were raised on Taco Bell and McDonald's, to the point where it became a weird "put this in your mouth and shut up" reward system. This particular chili was inspired by the filling of a Taco Bell Chili Cheese Burrito. It's just . . . SO GOOD, but you can't just order it as a chili! *Trust me, I've tried.* It has the same creaminess you remember, but without the mess of it falling out of a limp tortilla napkin.

1 tbsp (15 mL) olive oil

1 small onion, minced

1 tbsp (15 mL) cornstarch

2¼ cups (560 mL) water

¾ cup (175 mL) tomato paste

2 cups (500 mL) veggie ground beef

1 can (14 oz/398 mL) refried beans

1 jalapeño pepper, seeded and chopped

½ cup (125 mL) dairy-free Cheddar cheese shreds

1 tbsp (15 mL) chili powder

¼ tsp (1 mL) cayenne pepper

Sea salt

2 tsp (10 mL) white vinegar

OPTIONAL TOPPINGS

Dairy-free sour cream

Avocado–Ranch Sauce (see page 153)

Salsa

Chopped tomatoes

Chopped fresh cilantro

2 cups (500 mL) tortilla chips

1   In a medium saucepan, heat olive oil over medium-high heat. Add onion; cook, stirring occasionally, for 3 to 5 minutes, until translucent.

2   Meanwhile, in a small bowl, whisk together cornstarch and water.

3   Stir cornstarch mixture into the saucepan along with tomato paste. Add veggie ground beef, refried beans, jalapeño, dairy-free Cheddar cheese, chili powder, cayenne pepper, ½ tsp (2 mL) sea salt and white vinegar; stir to combine. Bring to a boil, then reduce heat to medium-low and simmer for 10 minutes, or until thickened and cheese is melted.

4   Season to taste with sea salt. Serve in bowls with toppings of choice and a side of tortilla chips (if using) for dipping or crushing and sprinkling over everything.

The first thing I did when I stopped eating meat was veganize classic fast food.

UDON OWN ME SOUP

SERVES 4

This sesame and miso soup packed with veggies and noodles is what I crave after a long rainy movie day. *The First Wives Club*, one of my faves, is a brilliant satire that tackles the sexism and ageism women experience in divorce. It ends with the leads dancing and singing Lesley Gore's "You Don't Own Me," about telling off a guy. What's this got to do with this soup? Nothing. I just wanted to remind you that when women and girls are educated and empowered, they lift up their entire community.

2 tbsp (30 mL) toasted sesame oil

4 green onions, white and green parts separated

2 garlic cloves, minced

2 tsp (10 mL) grated ginger

2 cups (500 mL) shredded green cabbage

2 carrots, sliced

Sea salt

1 bay leaf

3 cubes (each 1 tsp/5 mL) no-chicken or vegetable bouillon

6 cups (1.5 L) water

4 packages (each 7 oz/210 g) instant udon noodles

3 tbsp (45 mL) yellow or red miso paste

2 cups (500 mL) chopped bok choy

1 recipe Practically Perfect Crispy Tofu (page 180)

1 tbsp (15 mL) sesame seeds

I Put That Sh*t on Everything Chili Oil (page 196) or chili oil or hot sauce (optional)

1. In a medium saucepan, heat sesame oil over medium heat. Add the white parts of the green onions, garlic and ginger; cook for about 1 minute, until fragrant.

2. Add cabbage, carrots and a sprinkle of sea salt; cook for 2 to 3 minutes, until the vegetables begin to sweat. Add bay leaf, bouillon and water; bring to a boil. Reduce heat to medium-low, cover and simmer for 10 minutes, or until veggies are tender.

3. Meanwhile, cook udon noodles according to package instructions.

4. Transfer 1 cup (250 mL) broth from the saucepan to a small bowl. Add miso paste; stir until miso is completely dissolved. Add miso mixture to the saucepan.

5. Drain udon noodles and place in the saucepan along with the bok choy. Cook for 2 to 3 minutes, until heated through.

6. Remove bay leaf. Season to taste with sea salt. Divide soup among four bowls. Top with crispy tofu, the remaining green onions and sesame seeds. Serve on its own or with chili oil on the side (if using).

LABOR-SAVING LENTIL SOUP

SERVES 4 TO 6

When I need to empty my fridge, I make this lentil soup. It's absolute perfection just the way it is, but if you have any lingering greens, cauliflower, zucchini or tomato lying around, toss them in there, too. This recipe has become my go-to catch-all recipe for any veggies that need to be eaten up. Think of it as delicious recycling.

• ELECTRIC PRESSURE COOKER

2 tbsp (30 mL) olive oil

1 small onion, diced

3 garlic cloves, minced

Sea salt

2 carrots, chopped

2 stalks celery, chopped

1 cup (250 mL) dried red lentils, drained and rinsed

1 cup (250 mL) dried brown lentils, drained and rinsed

1 tbsp (15 mL) ground cumin

1 tsp (5 mL) dried thyme

1 tsp (5 mL) fennel seeds

1 tsp (5 mL) paprika

4 cubes (each 1 tsp/5 mL) no-chicken, no-beef or vegetable bouillon

6 cups (1.5 L) water (approx.)

1 tbsp (15 mL) tomato paste

1 bay leaf

1 can (14 oz/398 mL) full-fat coconut milk, divided

Freshly ground black pepper

3 tbsp (45 mL) chopped fresh parsley

1   In the electric pressure cooker, using the Sauté function on High, heat olive oil. Add onion, garlic and a pinch of sea salt; cook for 3 to 5 minutes, until onion is translucent. Add carrots and celery; cook for about 5 minutes, until the carrots are softened slightly.

2   Add red lentils, brown lentils, cumin, thyme, fennel seeds and paprika; cook for about 1 minute, until fragrant. Stir in bouillon, water, tomato paste and bay leaf; stir to combine.

3   Close the lid and cook on high pressure for 15 minutes. Let the pressure release naturally for 15 minutes. (Don't touch the cooker!) Quick-release the remaining pressure and open the lid.

4   Stir the soup and remove the bay leaf. Add 1 cup (250 mL) coconut milk (shake first to mix) and season to taste with sea salt and pepper. How thick or thin the soup is is really up to you. If you want a thinner soup, now's the time to add more water, a little bit at a time, to your liking.

5   Ladle soup into bowls. Divide the remaining coconut milk among the bowls and top with parsley. Serve with buttered toast alongside.

HACK IT!

Don't own a pressure cooker? Noooo problem! This recipe can be made easily on your stovetop in a large pot. Following the heating instructions, complete Steps 1 and 2, then bring the soup to a boil. Reduce heat to medium and simmer for 25 to 30 minutes, until the red lentils are soft and the brown lentils are tender but still hold their shape. Then complete Steps 4 and 5.

It's okay to be a lazy lentil!
I'm all about enjoying the
lentil things in life!

THERE'S AN APP FOR THAT

<u>th</u>erz \ ən \ ˈap \ fər, \ <u>th</u>at *(noun)*

1. A small portion of food (or drink) served before or at the beginning of a meal. *"Hey Suz, wanna split some apps, and get a couple mains to share? This menu looks unreal!"*

2. A short form of application. *"Dude, I just downloaded this TikTok app and I'm totally addicted!"*

3. A little taste of something that stimulates a desire for some extra or indicates more is to follow: *"Drinks were the app. Just wait 'til we get back to mine."*

~~~~~~

Apps, small plates, tapas, snacks: this chapter is jam-packed with tasty bites. Whether you need to satisfy a tiny rumble in your tum or stimulate your appetite before a big feast, I've got dips, chocolate bacon and fancy fries that are sure to amuse your bouche.

WHEN I CHIP, YOU CHIP, WE DIP

MAKES 3 CUPS (750 ML)

Warning: this onion dip may *ruffle* the feathers of your vegan friends. Inspired by French onion soup, this dip is just too rich to *not* be full of dairy. It's perfect for dipping chips, dunking veggies or using as a sandwich spread. While it may not be French cuisine, it is *très délicieuse*.

• HIGH-POWERED BLENDER

2 tbsp (30 mL) olive oil

1 large white or Spanish onion, diced

¾ tsp (3 mL) sea salt (approx.), divided

Water

1½ cups (375 mL) raw cashews, soaked (page 15), drained and rinsed

½ tsp (2 mL) garlic powder

½ tsp (2 mL) onion powder

¼ tsp (1 mL) white pepper

¾ cup (175 mL) egg-free mayo

1 tbsp (15 mL) freshly squeezed lemon juice

Potato chips (optional)

1. In a medium skillet, heat olive oil over medium-high heat. Add onion and ¼ tsp (1 mL) sea salt; cook, stirring constantly, for 10 to 15 minutes, until caramelized, adding water as needed to deglaze the pan if the onion is sticking or browning too quickly. Set aside to cool slightly.

2. In the high-powered blender, combine cashews, garlic powder, onion powder, white pepper, egg-free mayo, ½ cup (125 mL) water and lemon juice; blend on high speed until smooth.

3. Transfer cashew mixture to a medium airtight container. Stir in the cooled onion. Sprinkle in the remaining ½ tsp (2 mL) sea salt, stir and add more to taste. Refrigerate for at least 30 minutes or up to 5 days.

4. Just before serving, stir dip and place in your fanciest bowl. I like serving with plain potato chips for dipping, but you do you, boo.

PUFFED & STUFFED SPINACH PASTRIES

MAKES 2 DOZEN PASTRIES

What's better than a cheese- and spinach-stuffed pastry and an "I-eat-whatever-I-want" attitude? Not much. These spanakopita-inspired pinwheels are a first-class snack to serve to a crowd or eat all yourself (which I do). It also doesn't hurt that a lot of frozen puff pastry just happens to be vegan.

- **FOOD PROCESSOR**
- **2 RIMMED BAKING SHEETS LINED WITH PARCHMENT PAPER**

1 package (10 oz/300 g) frozen spinach, thawed

1 package (16 oz/450 g) extra-firm tofu, pressed (page 15) and coarsely chopped

1 tsp (5 mL) onion powder

1 tsp (5 mL) garlic powder

1 tsp (5 mL) dried basil

1 tsp (5 mL) dried parsley

½ tsp (2 mL) dried dill

½ tsp (2 mL) dried oregano

1 tbsp (15 mL) olive oil

2 tsp (10 mL) freshly squeezed lemon juice

2 tsp (10 mL) apple cider vinegar

1 garlic clove, minced

Sea salt

Pinch ground nutmeg

½ cup (125 mL) shredded dairy-free white cheese (optional)

2 tbsp (30 mL) unsweetened soy milk

1 tsp (5 mL) pure maple syrup

2 sheets (10 by 10 inches/ 25 by 25 cm) vegan-friendly puff pastry dough, thawed if frozen

1   Preheat the oven to 400°F (200°C).

2   Strain thawed spinach through a fine-mesh sieve or colander, squeezing out as much liquid as possible. Set aside.

3   In the food processor, combine tofu, onion powder, garlic powder, basil, parsley, dill, oregano, olive oil, lemon juice and apple cider vinegar. Pulse until pea-sized pieces form. Add spinach, garlic, ½ tsp (2 mL) sea salt and nutmeg; pulse to combine. Taste and season with additional sea salt if needed. Add dairy-free cheese (if using) and pulse to combine.

4   In a small bowl, whisk together soy milk and maple syrup. Set aside.

5   Roll out 1 puff pastry sheet to a 12-inch (30 cm) square. Spread half the spinach mixture onto the pastry. Working from the side closest to you, roll up the pastry and slice into twelve 1-inch (2.5 cm) thick pieces.

6   Transfer to a prepared baking sheet and brush the top of each slice with the maple syrup mixture. Repeat with the remaining puff pastry and spinach filling.

7   Bake in the preheated oven for about 15 minutes, until the pastry is puffed and golden brown. Transfer to a wire rack and let cool until cool enough to touch. Serve warm.

I'D LIKE S'AMORE GARLIC BREAD & PIZZA DIPPERS

SERVES 4 TO 6

I don't care who you are, buttery garlic bread with creamy garlic and jalapeño Cheddar dips will leave you belting "That's *amore*!" This classic American-Italian combo will always have a special place in my carb-loving heart. Sophisticated? No. Mouthwatering? You'd better believe it!

• RIMMED BAKING SHEET

GARLIC BREAD

½ cup (125 mL) dairy-free butter or margarine, softened

4 garlic cloves, grated

2 tbsp (30 mL) chopped flat-leaf (Italian) parsley, divided

1 tsp (5 mL) garlic powder

1 tsp (5 mL) Italian seasoning

¼ tsp (1 mL) sea salt

1 Italian loaf or French baguette, halved lengthwise

2 tsp (10 mL) chopped fresh chives

CREAMY GARLIC DIPPING SAUCE

½ cup (125 mL) egg-free mayo

1 tsp (5 mL) garlic powder

½ tsp (2 mL) Italian seasoning

1 tsp (5 mL) freshly squeezed lemon juice

Sea salt

JALAPEÑO CHEDDAR DIPPING SAUCE

1 tbsp (15 mL) dairy-free butter

¼ cup (60 mL) unsweetened soy milk

¼ cup (60 mL) dairy-free Cheddar cheese shreds

1 tbsp (15 mL) chopped pickled jalapeño peppers

Sea salt

---

1. Preheat the oven to 400°F (200°C).

2. **GARLIC BREAD** In a small bowl, combine softened dairy-free butter, garlic, 1 tbsp (15 mL) parsley, garlic powder, Italian seasoning and sea salt until smooth.

3. Place bread cut side up on the baking sheet. Spread garlic butter liberally on both cut sides of the bread. Bake in the preheated oven for 12 to 15 minutes, until the butter is bubbly and the bread is golden brown.

4. **CREAMY GARLIC DIPPING SAUCE** Meanwhile, in a small bowl, whisk together egg-free mayo, garlic powder, Italian seasoning and lemon juice. Season to taste with sea salt. Set aside.

5. **JALAPEÑO CHEDDAR DIPPING SAUCE** Meanwhile, in a small saucepan, melt dairy-free butter over medium heat. Stir in soy milk and bring to a gentle simmer, but do not boil. Add dairy-free Cheddar cheese, stirring constantly, until melted. Stir in jalapeños and season to taste with sea salt. Set aside.

6. Remove garlic bread from the oven and slice. Sprinkle with the remaining 1 tbsp (15 mL) parsley and chives. Serve with the dipping sauces, alongside pasta, lasagna or chili. Store dipping sauces in airtight containers in the fridge for up to 5 days.

With this sinner's snack, the only thing you'll need to beg forgiveness for is not making enough.

BEDEVILED POTATOES

MAKES 2 DOZEN POTATOES

This recipe has everything you love about deviled eggs . . . but uses potatoes instead. And since the devil is in the details, do not skip the black salt and an elegant sprinkling of paprika. These creamy two-bite wonders are tangy, a little sweet and satisfyingly piquant.

> • **STEAMER BASKET**
> • **BAKING SHEET**
> • **MELON BALLER (OPTIONAL)**
> • **POTATO RICER (OPTIONAL)**

12 baby yellow potatoes, halved

⅓ cup (75 mL) egg-free mayo

2 tbsp (30 mL) relish (sweet or dill)

1 tsp (5 mL) dairy-free butter or margarine, softened

1 tsp (5 mL) Dijon mustard

1 tsp (5 mL) garlic powder

½ tsp (2 mL) kala namak or seasoning salt

¼ tsp (1 mL) ground turmeric

¼ tsp (1 mL) freshly ground black pepper

1 to 2 tbsp (5 to 10 mL) unsweetened non-dairy milk of choice (optional)

Smoked paprika

Minced fresh chives or parsley (optional)

¼ cup (60 mL) simulated bacon bits (optional)

1 Fill a medium saucepan fitted with a steamer basket with 2 inches (5 cm) water and bring to a boil. Place potatoes in the basket and steam over medium-high heat for 15 to 20 minutes, until fork-tender. Using a slotted spoon, carefully transfer potatoes to the baking sheet until cool enough to handle.

2 Meanwhile, in a medium bowl, whisk together egg-free mayo, relish, dairy-free butter, Dijon, garlic powder, kala namak, turmeric and pepper.

3 Using the melon baller or a small spoon, gently scoop out the flesh of each potato half, being very careful not to pierce through the skin. Transfer potato flesh to a medium bowl and return the skins to the baking sheet.

4 Using the potato ricer (for an extra-smooth filling!) or fork, mash potatoes thoroughly, spreading out in the bowl until cooled completely.

5 Add mayo mixture to the potato and stir until it becomes a thick but velvety mash. If needed, add non-dairy milk 1 tbsp (15 mL) at a time, until smooth and creamy.

6 Using a melon baller or small spoon, gently spoon the potato mixture back into the potato skins. Sprinkle with paprika, chives and simulated bacon bits (if using). Serve as an hors d'oeuvre with Puffed & Stuffed Spinach Pastries (page 97) and Ostentatious Olives (page 105) at your next family reunion or brunch!

HACK IT!

Lighten your hosting load! Prep the potatoes and filling up to 24 hours in advance. Fill the skins just before serving.

Try different spices and seasonings for a variety of flavor profiles. Sometimes I use 1 tsp (5 mL) white wine vinegar instead of relish and add ¾ tsp (3 mL) curry powder, to make curried deviled eggs.

ACHIN' FOR SOME BACON-WRAPPED DATES

MAKES 1 DOZEN DATES

This appy is my ideal romantic partner: sweet, smoky, soft and vegan. If you can't find anyone who matches that description for yourself, don't worry, baby — there are 12 eggplant bacon-wrapped ones right here. Serve them at a party, and I promise there will be more dates in your future than dates on the plate.

- **RIMMED BAKING SHEET LINED WITH PARCHMENT PAPER**
- **12 TOOTHPICKS**

2 tbsp (30 mL) nutritional yeast

2 tsp (10 mL) garlic powder

¼ tsp (1 mL) freshly ground black pepper

¼ tsp (1 mL) paprika

3 tbsp (45 mL) tamari or soy sauce

2 tbsp (30 mL) olive oil

2 tsp (10 mL) pure maple syrup

½ tsp (2 mL) liquid smoke

¼ medium eggplant, peeled, quartered lengthwise and very thinly sliced

2 tbsp (30 mL) soft dairy-free cheese (try my Mixed Herb & Garlic Chèvre, page 111)

12 large Medjool dates, pitted and sliced open

1. Preheat the oven to 325°F (160°C).

2. In a small bowl, whisk together nutritional yeast, garlic powder, pepper, paprika, tamari, olive oil, maple syrup and liquid smoke.

3. Brush both sides of the eggplant slices with tamari marinade. Arrange in a single layer on the prepared baking sheet.

4. Bake in the preheated oven for 20 minutes, flip and bake for another 5 minutes, or until lightly browned (reserve baking sheet). Transfer to a wire rack to cool slightly. Increase oven temperature to 400°F (200°C).

5. Meanwhile, spoon a small amount of dairy-free cheese into the cavity of each date and press shut.

6. Cut the eggplant slices in half. Wrap one eggplant half around each date and secure with a toothpick. Place on the reserved baking sheet, date and cheese side up.

7. Bake in the preheated oven for 10 minutes, or until dates have darkened slightly and eggplant is crisping.

8. Remove from the oven and let cool slightly. Transfer to a serving platter and serve warm or at room temperature with a cheeky bottle of red wine.

SALT & VINEGAR EDAMAME

SERVES 4 TO 6

The first sake bomb I ever had was on a trip to Miami with my vegan Instagram girlfriends. Nothing bonds you with internet pals you've never met quite like chanting in a sushi restaurant and spilling Japanese beer all over your dress, right? The only thing I took back to my hotel room that night was the salt and vinegar edamame, and I think you'll love this simple snack just as much as I do.

> • RIMMED BAKING SHEET LINED WITH PARCHMENT PAPER

2 cups (500 mL) white vinegar

1 package (16 oz/450 g) frozen edamame

1 tbsp (15 mL) olive oil

Flakey sea salt and freshly ground black pepper

1 Preheat the oven to broil.

2 In a medium saucepan, bring white vinegar to a boil. Remove pan from heat, add edamame and let stand for 7 minutes.

3 Drain edamame. Toss with olive oil and ¼ tsp (1 mL) flakey sea salt.

4 Spread edamame in a single layer on the prepared baking sheet. Broil on the top rack for 1 to 2 minutes, until you see some charred bits.

5 Sprinkle with flakey sea salt and pepper to taste. Serve hot.

OSTENTATIOUS OLIVES

MAKES 1½ CUPS (375 ML)

Need a fancy app for fancy friends? This is one of my favorite easy ways to show off, and it can be made in less time than it takes you to put on your diamond-encrusted tennis bracelet. Even if you accidentally invited one of those weird olive haters, I bet even they'll be cured. These are perfect alongside a glass of wine, a sunset and some bread to sop up the herbed oil.

¼ cup (60 mL) olive oil

2 garlic cloves, sliced

1 small fresh rosemary sprig or ½ tsp (2 mL) dried rosemary

1 tsp (5 mL) grated lemon zest

½ tsp (2 mL) red pepper flakes

1 cup (250 mL) black or green olives

1 tbsp (15 mL) chopped fresh parsley

⅛ tsp (0.5 mL) flakey sea salt

1 In a medium saucepan, combine olive oil, garlic, rosemary, lemon zest and red pepper flakes. Bring to a simmer over medium heat. Reduce heat to medium-low and simmer gently, stirring occasionally, for 4 to 6 minutes, until garlic is golden but not browned. Remove from heat and add the olives. Let stand for 15 minutes.

2 Sprinkle with parsley and flakey sea salt. Serve warm, alongside your favorite dairy-free fancy cheese, baguette and a small dish for the pits.

BUILDING A BRIE-LLIANT CHARCUTERIE BOARD

I am all about romanticizing our lives a bit more, *especially now that we're allowed out of our houses! Anyone else have residual Covid-19 PTSD?* This may look like a ladies' picnic, a sensual date by the lake or hosting a summer soirée in the backyard. What I don't love is lots of planning, piles of dishes and being stuck in the kitchen while everyone else is having a fabulous time. *Boooo!* So, over the last few years, I have learned to master the art of a chic vegan charcuterie board. Easily prepped in advance, my fuss-free snack board has minimal cleanup and is easy to put together while at the same time looking fresh, impressively bountiful and artfully high-end. Catching up with your guests — drinks in hand — sounds *wayyyy* better than sweating over the stove, doesn't it?

Traditionally, these boards are filled with arranged meats, cheese, crudités, seasonal fruit and even flowers (you've probably seen it on the 'gram). At this point you may be thinking, "Candice, without all that, isn't it just a veggie platter?" *But stay with me!* So many gorgeous plant-based alternatives to meat and dairy are now available that you can create a max snack board without ever having to compromise on taste, texture or flavor. Let me show you how.

continues on page 108 ⟶

STEP 1: THE PERFECT SURFACE

You're going to need something to arrange this artwork on. Any interesting table, large marble slab, wooden board or silver tray will work — or even a concrete countertop. I like to tailor my surface to my decor or event theme (think garden party, casual cocktails, farmhouse vibe, etc.), but most often I use a thrifted large wooden board. Cheap and cheerful!

STEP 2: THE FOOD

The key to magazine-worthy charcuterie boards is variety. No one wants a table full of brown and beige sameness.

Fruit & Veg You know what's great about Mother Nature? Color! Choose items that are varied in shape, texture and shades, as well as plenty of dippable items. And highlight in-season fruit and veg — my usual suspects are grapes, strawberries, blueberries, apple, pineapple and even dried fruit like figs and apricots, along with cherry tomatoes, carrot sticks, bell peppers and cucumbers.

Plant-Based Cheese & Dips Thanks to the rise of interest in plant-based living, we have a wonderful variety of dairy-free cheeses available at most supermarkets. However, if you want something specific, you may have to hit a specialty store. Applying the same principles as mentioned above, I like to choose a variety of textures and flavors. A neutral soft goat-like or Brie-like cheese such as my Mixed Herb & Garlic Chèvre (page 111) is a must, but you want to also include some aged flavors, dairy-free Cheddar cheese cubes or — my favorite — a truffled cheese spread. In addition to dairy-free cheese, you can use a variety of spreads and dips like hummus, spinach dip and vegan pâtés.

Plant-Based Protein Now pay attention, because this is where a lot of folks go wrong. The biggest mistake I see with plant-based charcuterie boards is a lack of protein. (*See, I told you this wasn't going to be a veggie platter!*) You can include premade items like smoked tofu, sliced plant-based sausage, veggie cold cuts, thinly sliced seitan and smoked carrot lox. Remember: variety, variety, variety!

Carbs, Carbs, Carbs This should be a no-brainer, but then, this morning I saw some betch on TikTok put SANDWICH BREAD on a grazing board. *Girl! Who hurt you?! This is not a garden party hosted in a parking lot.* Wonder Bread is an emphatic no. Acceptable carbs on your board include sturdy, crusty breads such as baguette, two types of crackers, breadsticks, potato chips and baguette crisps.

Finishing Touches A variety of nuts, jellies, preserves, jams and pickled items completes the experience. Nothing rounds out the perfect board like a hot pepper jelly, blueberry preserve, olives, tiny gherkins and/or pickled onions. I like to look at it as if I am giving my friends the opportunity to build sophisticated "snackables" with luxurious garnishes.

STEP 3: PLATING

A. Arrange your dips, spreads and bowls of accompaniments on the platter first.

B. Next, place the proteins in small piles in two different areas of the board. If you are using veggie cold cuts, try folding them in an interesting way before you put them down.

C. Place the cheeses in any large gaps on the board — and don't forget to provide a cheese knife for each.

D. Fill other empty spaces with your carbs of choice in neat rows or short jars or glasses.

E. Lay down the produce, creating movement and filling any empty space. Use a combination of neat rows and irregular piles, depending on the item, and distribute them across the board instead of grouping like items with like items. We want it to be full of variety without any empty spots.

F. Fill in any remaining gaps with garnishes like small piles of nuts, edible flowers and fresh herbs. Take a look, adjust as needed, then you're ready to serve! Look at you go, you fancy little minx, you!

FANCY FALL CHARCUTERIE BOARD

SERVES 4 TO 6

A beautiful grazing board that looks like it stepped right out of Insta can seem a bit intimidating. I get it. I felt the same way when these gorgeous spreads became all the rage. But I found that picking a theme or season often helps spark my creativity, and what's the coziest, prettiest season of them all? Fall. So, here's some help with an autumn harvest–inspired board to make you look like a modern June Cleaver in less than 15 minutes.

• 2 CHEESE KNIVES

¾ **cup (175 mL)** prepared hummus

3 tbsp (45 mL) Dijon mustard

3 tbsp (45 mL) apple butter

2 plant-based Italian sausages, cooked and sliced

6 oz (175 g) smoked tofu, sliced

6 oz (175 g) dairy-free Brie wheel

6 oz (175 g) dairy-free aged Cheddar cheese, cubed

8 breadsticks

1 bunch red grapes

10 baby rainbow carrots

12 cranberry and seed crackers

12 baguette slices, toasted

⅔ **cup (150 mL)** mixed nuts

Fresh rosemary sprigs (optional but really pretty!)

1 Put hummus, Dijon and apple butter into a nice small bowl each and place on different areas of the board. Place a tiny spoon in each.

2 Lay down plant-based sausage and smoked tofu. I like to put them in little rows on two sides of the board.

3 Add dairy-free cheeses, arranging the dairy-free Brie and Cheddar cheeses next to condiments. Place a cheese knife beside each.

4 Arrange breadsticks in a short jar or glass so they stand upright. Next, place grapes in one area of the board. If they're quite large, you can halve them and arrange in opposite areas. Place carrots, crackers and baguette slices anywhere there is an empty space.

5 Place little piles of nuts all over the board to fill up any remaining space. Drape rosemary sprigs artfully across the board to garnish (if using). Success!

MIXED HERB & GARLIC CHÈVRE

MAKES ¾ CUP (175 ML)

Fancy vegan cheese can cost up to $20 for a piece no larger than the palm of my hand. Now, only if there were a way to throw $3 worth of pantry staples into a food processor and make your own artisanal herb and garlic chèvre . . .

• FOOD PROCESSOR

8 oz (225 g) extra-firm tofu, pressed (page 15) and coarsely chopped

¾ tsp (3 mL) sea salt

½ tsp (2 mL) onion powder

½ tsp (2 mL) garlic powder

2 tsp (10 mL) refined coconut oil (approx.), melted

1 tsp (5 mL) freshly squeezed lemon juice

1 tsp (5 mL) apple cider vinegar

1¼ tsp (6 mL) dried basil, divided

1¼ tsp (6 mL) dried parsley, divided

1 tsp (5 mL) dried dill, divided

1 tsp (5 mL) dried oregano, divided

1. In the food processor, place tofu; process until crumbled, stopping the motor and scraping down the sides of the bowl as needed. Add sea salt, onion powder, garlic powder, coconut oil, lemon juice and apple cider vinegar; process until a smooth ball forms. If the mixture does not come together easily, add an additional 1 tsp (5 mL) coconut oil at a time until it does.

2. Using your hands, break the ball up in the food processor bowl and sprinkle in ½ tsp (2 mL) basil, ½ tsp (2 mL) parsley, ¼ tsp (1 mL) dill and ¼ tsp (1 mL) oregano overtop. Pulse to combine.

3. In a small bowl, combine the remaining basil, remaining parsley, remaining dill and remaining oregano. Set aside.

4. On a clean surface, scoop out tofu mixture and form it into a log about 6 inches (15 cm) long and 4 inches (10 cm) wide. Lay down a large piece of parchment paper or plastic wrap and sprinkle with the reserved herb mixture. Gently roll the tofu in the herbs to coat the sides completely. Tightly wrap up tofu in the parchment paper and place in the fridge to chill for at least 30 minutes or up to 1 week.

5. Plate alongside your favorite crackers, veggies and fruit (check out my charcuterie board guide on page 106) or crumble over salads.

HACK IT!

I like to make this the night before I need it, giving the flavors lots of time to meld.

BEAN CHEESIN' TACOS DORADOS

SERVES 4

I had this friend in college who made taquitos as a snack by tossing cheese onto a tortilla and heating it in the microwave. *Sir? Are you okay?!* While he was somewhat on the right track, taquitos (aka Mexican tacos dorados) deserve better. Heck, *we* deserve better. We deserve a taco! But rolled! And crispy! Filled to the brim with cheese and hearty refried beans, with salsa on the side. Now, *that's* a snack.

- **HIGH-POWERED BLENDER**
- **2 RIMMED BAKING SHEETS LINED WITH PARCHMENT PAPER AND GREASED**
- **20 TOOTHPICKS (OPTIONAL)**

1 small yellow potato, peeled and cubed

½ cup (125 mL) vegan sour cream

¼ cup (60 mL) tomato salsa

1 jalapeño pepper, seeded and minced

2 cups (500 mL) veggie ground beef

1 package (1 oz/30 g) taco seasoning

⅓ cup (75 mL) raw cashews

1 tbsp (15 mL) nutritional yeast

¼ tsp (1 mL) ground cumin

¼ tsp (1 mL) ground turmeric

⅓ cup (75 mL) vegetable broth

¼ cup (60 mL) sliced pickled green chiles, drained

1 tbsp (15 mL) pickled green chile juice

Sea salt

20 small corn tortillas

1¾ cups + 1 tbsp (440 mL) refried beans

Cooking spray or 3 tbsp (45 mL) olive oil

1. Preheat the oven to 350°F (180°C).

2. Place potato cubes in a small saucepan and cover with 1 inch (2.5 cm) water. Bring to a boil, cover and cook for 10 to 15 minutes, until soft. Using a glass measuring cup, scoop out ¼ cup (60 mL) cooking water and set aside. Drain potatoes and place in the high-powered blender. Let cool slightly.

3. In a small bowl, combine vegan sour cream, salsa and jalapeño. Set aside.

4. Heat a medium skillet over medium heat. Add veggie ground beef, taco seasoning and ¾ cup (175 mL) water. Cook for about 5 minutes, until thickened and water has evaporated. Set aside.

5. To the blender, add cashews, nutritional yeast, cumin, turmeric, broth, pickled green chiles and juice. Blend on high speed until smooth, adding 1 tbsp (15 mL) cooking water at a time until creamy and spreadable. Season to taste with sea salt. Voilà! You have made queso!

6. Wrap tortillas in damp paper towel. Microwave on High in 15-second intervals until warm.

7. Spread about 1½ tbsp (22 mL) refried beans in the center of each tortilla. Top with about 1½ tbsp (22 mL) veggie ground beef and evenly divide the queso. Tightly roll tortillas, securing each with a toothpick if needed. Place on the prepared baking sheets, seam side down, spacing ½ inch (1 cm) apart.

8. Spray the tops of the rolled tortillas with cooking spray or brush lightly with olive oil. Bake in the preheated oven for 12 to 15 minutes, flipping halfway, until the edges of tortillas are golden.

9. Remove the toothpicks (if you used them) and serve warm on a platter with the creamy salsa dip.

HACK IT!

There are so many yummy variations of this recipe. Try filling the tacos with your favorite plant-based chicken strips instead of the veggie ground beef and/ or adding ½ cup (125 mL) guacamole to the dip.

SMOKY CHOCOLATE-COVERED BAE-CON

MAKES 20 PIECES

A couple years ago, a well-known blogger shared my rice paper bacon recipe (see my first book) and broke the internet. It was trolled by some, but loved by most. So, five years later, as a treat to those same people, I've created an unconventional, sort-of-dessert version that will delight your guests as a savory-sweet app.

• 2 RIMMED BAKING SHEETS LINED WITH PARCHMENT PAPER

¼ **cup (60 mL)** nutritional yeast

1 **tbsp (15 mL)** garlic powder

½ **tsp (2 mL)** freshly ground black pepper

½ **tsp (2 mL)** paprika

6 **tbsp (90 mL)** tamari or soy sauce

¼ **cup (60 mL)** olive oil

1 **tbsp (15 mL)** pure maple syrup

½ **tsp (2 mL)** liquid smoke or 1 tbsp (15 mL) vegan-friendly BBQ sauce

Ten 9-inch (23 cm) rice paper wrappers

Twenty 8-inch (20 cm) skewers, soaked if wood

1½ **cups (375 mL)** dairy-free semisweet chocolate chips

1 **tbsp (15 mL)** coconut oil

1½ **tbsp (22 mL)** sea salt

1   Preheat the oven to 400°F (200°C).

2   In a medium bowl, whisk together nutritional yeast, garlic powder, pepper, paprika, tamari, olive oil, maple syrup and liquid smoke. Set aside.

3   Fill a large bowl with warm water.

4   Place one rice paper wrapper over another, two-ply style, and quickly dip the layered rice paper wrapper into warm water to soften slightly. Place on a large cutting board.

5   Using sharp scissors, cut the layered rice paper into 1½-inch (4 cm) wide strips. You should be able to get 4 to 5 strips. Repeat with the remaining rice paper.

6   One at a time, dip the layered strips of rice paper into the tamari marinade. Thread each strip onto its own skewer and place on the prepared baking sheets. Repeat with the remaining rice paper strips, whisking the marinade every so often to prevent separation.

7   Bake in the preheated oven for 7 to 8 minutes, until crisp. The strips burn easily, so keep an eye on them. Transfer skewers to a wire rack to cool completely. Reserve baking sheets and line with clean parchment paper.

8   Meanwhile, place chocolate in a small microwave-safe bowl. Microwave on High in 30-second intervals, stirring in between, until melted. Stir in coconut oil.

9   Brush each side of the rice paper bacon with melted chocolate and place on the baking sheets. Sprinkle with sea salt and refrigerate until firm, about 1 hour. You can make these in advance and store for up to 3 days.

FREESTYLE FRIES

SERVES 4

One of my favorite recipes from my first book is the Kimchi Fries, and it would be a crime against, well, myself if I didn't include another ridiculous fry concoction. This one is inspired by Chinese freestyle fries (*guailu yangyu* in Mandarin), a popular street food from the Guizhou province of China, just without the animal products. It's the perfect combination of spicy, salty, sweet and sour that you have to taste for yourself to believe.

1½ packages (each 1 lb/500 g) frozen French fries

FREESTYLE MAYO

¼ cup (60 mL) egg-free mayo

¼ tsp (1 mL) garlic powder

1 tbsp (15 mL) sambal oelek

1 tsp (5 mL) seasoned rice vinegar

TOPPINGS

1 tsp (5 mL) seasoning salt

¼ cup (60 mL) vegetarian hoisin sauce

⅓ cup (75 mL) unsalted chopped peanuts

¼ cup (60 mL) pickled onion

3 green onions, finely chopped

3 tbsp (45 mL) chopped fresh cilantro

1 lime, quartered

1 Prepare French fries according to package instructions.

2 **FREESTYLE MAYO** Meanwhile, in a small bowl, whisk together egg-free mayo, garlic powder, sambal oelek and rice vinegar. Set aside.

3 Remove fries from the oven and transfer to a serving dish. Sprinkle with seasoning salt and drizzle with vegetarian hoisin sauce. Top with peanuts, pickled onion, green onions and cilantro. Serve with freestyle mayo and lime wedges.

SOUTHERN-STYLE POPCORN BITES

SERVES 4

Tender on the inside and crispy on the outside, these morsels of magic came to me out of necessity after KFC stopped serving its vegan version of popcorn chicken. Does it taste like the Colonel's? Nope. It's better. Serve with my Jerk Aioli (see page 148) for a little extra sumthin'.

- **DEEP FRYER OR HEAVY-BOTTOMED SAUCEPAN FITTED WITH A DEEP-FRY THERMOMETER**
- **WIRE RACK OVER A RIMMED BAKING SHEET**

5 cubes (each 1 tsp/5 mL) no-chicken or vegetable bouillon

3 cups (750 mL) boiling water

1½ cups (375 mL) dry soy curls

⅓ cup (75 mL) aquafaba (page 15), whisked until foamy

1 tbsp (15 mL) soy sauce

⅓ cup (75 mL) cornstarch, divided

¾ cup (175 mL) unbleached all-purpose flour

2 tbsp (30 mL) paprika

1 tbsp (15 mL) garlic powder

1 tbsp (15 mL) white pepper

1½ tsp (7 mL) dry mustard powder

1½ tsp (7 mL) ground ginger

1 tsp (5 mL) dried thyme

1 tsp (5 mL) dried basil

1 tsp (5 mL) MSG or sea salt (optional)

½ tsp (2 mL) baking soda

½ tsp (2 mL) baking powder

½ tsp (2 mL) dried oregano

½ tsp (2 mL) celery salt

½ tsp (2 mL) freshly ground black pepper

Vegetable oil

1. In a large bowl, whisk together bouillon and boiling water until dissolved. Stir in soy curls. Set aside to soak for 10 minutes, or until very soft and doubled in size.

2. Using your hands, squeeze out as much liquid as you can from the soy curls, then transfer to a cutting board. Cut soy curls into roughly 1½-inch (4 cm) bites and place in a large bowl.

3. To the large bowl, add aquafaba and soy sauce; toss to coat. Add 1 tbsp (15 mL) cornstarch and toss to coat. Set aside.

4. In a separate large bowl, combine flour, the remaining ¼ cup (60 mL) cornstarch, paprika, garlic powder, white pepper, mustard powder, ginger, thyme, basil, MSG (if using), baking soda, baking powder, oregano, celery salt and black pepper.

5. Into the deep fryer or a heavy-bottomed saucepan, pour oil to at least 3 inches (7.5 cm). Heat vegetable oil to between 350°F (180°C) and 375°F (190°C).

6. Give soy curls a quick toss in the aquafaba mixture and then toss in the flour mixture, pressing down gently to help the flour stick to the curls. Dust off any excess and place on the wire rack.

7. Working in batches, fry soy curls in hot oil, turning two to three times, for 3 to 4 minutes, until golden brown. Do not overcrowd or else they will not cook properly. Transfer soy curls to the prepared wire rack to allow excess oil to drip off. Let the oil return to between 350°F (180°C) and 375°F (190°C) between batches.

8. Place popcorn bites in a serving dish and serve alongside your favorite dips, or add to salads, I'm Drunk! Noodles! (page 157) or Massaman-Style Tofu Curry (page 154) for a little extra oomph.

THINGS THAT MAKE YOU GO MMM-MAINS

thiŋs \ <u>th</u>at \ māk \ yü \ gō \ mmm-mānz *(noun)*

1. An expression used to show contentment for an exceptional meal. *"Mmm, this gnocchi is incredible! Could you give me another helping?"*

2. That questionable sound you make when you see or hear something that gets you excited. *"Mmm, that sounds wonderful."*

We all love to eat, but we don't all love to cook. And some of us love to cook but don't want to spend hours in the kitchen after work or stressing before a crowd shows up for dinner. That is why in the next few pages you will find mains that dazzle without too much effort. Delicious one-pot wonders, meals to impress, work lunches you'll look forward to and dinner in under 15 minutes. Make sure to check out the *Hack It!* features for variations and leftover tips!

LAZY LASAGNA

SERVES 4 TO 6

I'm a Taurus, which means that I am a workhorse, but like, *so* lazy. Don't ask me how that makes sense (I'm not convinced it does), because I'm literally too lazy to find out. This life of mine is run with a "laziness is the first step to efficiency" mentality, and an "if I can't reach it, I don't need it" work ethic. So, if you want lasagna, but like, "ugh . . . so many layers and steps," this recipe is for you.

• 13- BY 9-INCH (33 BY 23 CM) CASSEROLE DISH

2 tbsp (30 mL) olive oil

3 small carrots, diced

3 stalks celery, diced

Sea salt

2 cups (500 mL) veggie ground beef

2 tbsp (30 mL) Italian seasoning

½ tsp (2 mL) onion powder

½ tsp (2 mL) garlic powder

½ tsp (2 mL) freshly ground black pepper

Red pepper flakes (optional)

2 jars (each 26 oz/700 mL) marinara sauce

½ cup (125 mL) water

1 cube (1 tsp/5 mL) no-beef or vegetable bouillon

11 oven-ready lasagna noodles, broken into bite-sized pieces

3 cups (750 mL) chopped spinach

½ cup (125 mL) unsweetened soy milk

3 cups (750 mL) dairy-free mozzarella cheese shreds, divided

¼ cup (60 mL) chopped flat-leaf (Italian) parsley

1 Preheat the oven to 400°F (200°C).

2 In a large pot, heat olive oil over medium-high heat. Add carrots, celery and a pinch of sea salt; cook for 3 to 5 minutes, until softened slightly. Stir in veggie ground beef, Italian seasoning, onion powder, garlic powder, pepper and a pinch of red pepper flakes (if using); cook for 2 minutes, or until heated through.

3 Add marinara sauce, water and bouillon; bring to a boil. Reduce heat to medium and stir in the broken lasagna noodles, spinach and soy milk. Cover and simmer for 5 minutes, stirring frequently, or until the liquid has thickened slightly and the lasagna noodles are beginning to soften.

4 Stir in 1 cup (250 mL) dairy-free mozzarella cheese and transfer the lasagna mixture to the casserole dish. Spread out the mixture in an even layer and top with the remaining 2 cups (500 mL) dairy-free mozzarella cheese. Cover with foil.

5 Bake in the preheated oven for 15 minutes. Uncover and bake for another 5 to 10 minutes, until cheese has melted, sauce is bubbly and lasagna noodles are tender.

6 Transfer to a wire rack and let stand for 5 minutes.

7 Serve garnished with fresh parsley and red pepper flakes (if using).

HACK IT!

So many amazing gluten-free lasagna noodles are out there now! So go ahead and grab some — no need to miss out just because you're celiac.

Like poutine, this humble Canadian dish is satisfying, but we git'r done and finish every bite.

BLUENOSIN' DONAIRS

SERVES 4

When people think of Canadian cuisine, they often think poutine, the Quebec classic. But this East Coast staple should also be on your radar. A traditional donair consists of heavily spiced, spit-roasted and shaved beef on a Lebanese-style pita, topped with tomatoes, raw onions and a drizzle of sweet, garlicky sauce. I've swapped the beef for meaty soy curls, but kept ALL the other delicious fillings.

• GRILL PAN (OPTIONAL)

½ **cup (125 mL)** egg-free mayo

2½ **tbsp (37 mL)** organic granulated sugar

1½ **tsp (7 mL)** garlic powder, divided

1½ **tbsp (22 mL)** white vinegar

3 **cubes (each 1 tsp/5 mL)** no-beef or vegetable bouillon

4 **cups (1 L)** boiling water

4 **cups (1 L)** dry soy curls

3 **tbsp (45 mL)** vegan-friendly BBQ sauce

2 **tbsp (30 mL)** soy sauce

2 **tbsp (30 mL)** pure maple syrup

¾ **tsp (3 mL)** olive oil

½ **tsp (2 mL)** dried oregano

¼ **tsp (1 mL)** Italian seasoning

¼ **tsp (1 mL)** cayenne pepper

¼ **tsp (1 mL)** freshly ground black pepper

4 large Lebanese-style pitas

1 small white onion, diced

2 plum (Roma) tomatoes, diced

¼ **cup (60 mL)** chopped fresh parsley

1 In a small bowl, whisk together egg-free mayo, sugar and 1 tsp (5 mL) garlic powder. Very slowly pour in white vinegar, whisking constantly to combine. You've made donair sauce! Place in the fridge while you prepare the rest of the recipe.

2 In a large bowl, dissolve bouillon in 4 cups (1 L) boiling water. Add soy curls, stir to combine and then let stand for 10 minutes.

3 Meanwhile, fill a large pot halfway with water and bring to a boil.

4 In a separate large bowl, whisk together BBQ sauce, soy sauce, maple syrup, olive oil, the remaining ½ tsp (2 mL) garlic powder, oregano, Italian seasoning, cayenne pepper and pepper. Set aside.

5 Remove soy curls from the bowl (discarding liquid). Using your hands, squeeze out all excess liquid. Place soy curls in the bowl with the spice mixture; toss to coat.

6 Heat the grill pan or a large skillet over medium-high heat. Add soy curls and cook for 7 to 10 minutes, until heated through and browned.

7 Wrap pitas in damp paper towel. Microwave on High for 45 to 60 seconds, until soft and fluffy.

8 On each pita, lay down soy curls and top with onion and tomatoes. Drizzle with donair sauce and sprinkle with parsley; serve.

BABY BACK, BABY BACK, BABY BACK RIB SAMMY

SERVES 4

GET IN MY BELLY!!! This finger-lickin' plant-based take on McDonald's cult favorite is as drool-worthy as it is messy. Juicy, tender mushrooms tossed in BBQ sauce are topped with tangy pickles and onion, then sandwiched in a soft white roll. I mean, if anyone comes at you with "If there are no ribs in it, it can't be a McRib," kindly remind them that McDonald's ribs aren't even ribs and to mind their manners. Then get yourself some napkins, smother this thing in sawse and indulge like a bawse.

3 tbsp (45 mL) balsamic vinegar

1 cup + 2 tbsp (280 mL) vegan-friendly BBQ sauce, divided

2 tbsp (30 mL) olive oil

8 large portobello mushrooms, stems removed

Four 6-inch (15 cm) hoagie-style rolls, halved

8 dill pickle medallions

½ cup (125 mL) sliced white onion

1 In a large sealable container or shallow bowl, whisk together balsamic vinegar, 2 tbsp (30 mL) BBQ sauce and olive oil.

2 Brush marinade all over the mushrooms until coated completely. Position mushrooms, gill side up, in the marinade and let stand for a minimum of 10 minutes or up to 24 hours, covered, in the fridge. The longer they marinate, the stronger their flavor will be.

3 Heat a large skillet over medium-high heat and pour in about half the marinade. Working in batches (I usually cook 4 at a time), add the mushrooms, gill side down, and cook for 2 to 3 minutes, until the liquid begins to release. Reduce heat to medium. Using a heavy pan or pot that fits inside your skillet, flatten mushrooms by pressing down gently. Cook for 2 to 3 minutes. Flip mushrooms, flatten again and cook for another 2 to 3 minutes, until tender.

4 Flip mushrooms so they are gill side down again. Increase heat to medium-high. Cook for 3 to 5 minutes, until the liquid has evaporated. Repeat with the remaining mushrooms, adjusting heat and adding marinade between batches as necessary. (If you want to get super copy-catty, remove mushrooms from the skillet after cooking and trim into long thick rectangles to resemble the shape of the McDonald's sandwich.)

5 Meanwhile, in a large shallow bowl, place the remaining 1 cup (250 mL) BBQ sauce. Set aside.

6   Preheat the oven to broil. Place rolls on a baking sheet. Broil on the top rack for about 1 minute, until golden brown. Watch carefully so they don't burn! Set aside. (If you want a warm, soft bun, skip the broiling, complete Step 7 and microwave each assembled sandwich on High for 15 seconds.)

7   Dip each mushroom into the BBQ sauce, ensuring it's completely coated; shake off excess. Place 2 mushrooms on the bottom half of each roll, followed by 2 pickle medallions, sliced onion and the bun top.

HACK IT!

This stew can be enjoyed in several ways. Instead of noods, try it with creamy mashed potatoes or even cooked rice. And if you're gluten-free, just swap regular noodles for a gluten-free version.

Is your local grocer sold out of veggie beef chunks? No problem! Sub in the same amount of cooked, cubed tofu or mushrooms.

NO-BULL BOEUF BOURGUIGNON

SERVES 4 TO 6

This is my interpretation of the iconic French beef stew with perfectly braised onions and mushrooms in a dark red wine sauce. Before Julia Child introduced it to us Jell-O-salad-eating North Americans, the dish was considered peasant food and often enjoyed by travelers staying at the inn. Since learning this, I straight up can't make this without picturing a wench singing "My broth bringeth all the gentlefolk to my yard." Aaaand this is why I shouldn't be allowed to watch *Outlander*.

3 tbsp (45 mL) dairy-free butter or margarine

1 tbsp (15 mL) olive oil

16 oz (500 g) sliced mixed mushrooms, such as cremini, portobello and porcini

4 tsp (20 mL) minced garlic, divided

4 cubes (each 1 tsp/5 mL) no-beef or vegetable bouillon, crushed

3 cups (750 mL) hot water

2 large carrots, sliced

½ large white onion, diced

½ cup (125 mL) oil-packed sun-dried tomatoes, halved and sliced

1 tsp (5 mL) Italian seasoning

1 tsp (5 mL) dried thyme

Freshly ground black pepper

Sea salt

¼ cup (60 mL) unbleached all-purpose flour

2 tbsp (30 mL) tomato paste

8 pearl onions (optional)

2 cups (500 mL) red wine

4 cups (1 L) vegetarian beef chunks

1 tsp (5 mL) liquid smoke

1 bay leaf

1 lb (500 g) fettucine or egg-free pappardelle

1 tbsp (15 mL) finely chopped fresh parsley

1. In a large saucepan or Dutch oven, heat dairy-free butter and olive oil over high heat. Add mushrooms and 2 tsp (10 mL) garlic; cook, stirring occasionally, for about 5 minutes, until mushrooms release their liquid.

2. Meanwhile, in a small bowl, combine bouillon and hot water. Stir to dissolve the bouillon; set aside.

3. To the saucepan, add carrots, white onion, sun-dried tomatoes, remaining 2 tsp (10 mL) garlic, Italian seasoning, thyme, ¼ tsp (1 mL) pepper and a sprinkle of sea salt; cook, stirring occasionally, for 3 to 5 minutes, until onion is translucent.

4. Add flour and tomato paste; cook, stirring constantly, for 3 to 4 minutes, until thickened. Add pearl onions (if using) and red wine; bring to a boil. Boil for about 3 minutes, stirring constantly, until you no longer smell the alcohol. Add vegetarian beef chunks, bouillon mixture, liquid smoke and bay leaf; cover and bring to a boil. Reduce heat to medium-low and simmer for 20 minutes, stirring occasionally, or until the flavors have melded and the liquid has reduced slightly.

5. Meanwhile, bring a large pot of salted water to a boil. Cook pasta according to package instructions. Using a glass measuring cup, scoop out ½ cup (125 mL) pasta water and set aside. Drain pasta and cover the colander with a pot lid.

6. Remove bay leaf from the saucepan and add reserved pasta water. Season to taste with sea salt and pepper. Divide pasta evenly among four to six plates and top with bourg; garnish with parsley.

NO REGRETTI BOLOGNESE SPAGHETTI

SERVES 4 TO 6

I am a firm believer that the world would be a much happier place if we all just shut the eff up and embraced carbs. What did carbs ever do to any of us? Carbs are life; carbs are happiness. And if I wanted to hate myself, I would just look at my bank account.

2 tbsp (30 mL) olive oil

1 small onion, diced

3 garlic cloves, minced

1 lb (500 g) veggie ground beef

½ cup (125 mL) unsweetened soy milk

1 can (28 oz/796 mL) diced tomatoes (with juice)

1 tbsp (15 mL) dried oregano

Sea salt

Freshly ground black pepper

1 lb (500 g) spaghetti

Grated dairy-free Parmesan cheese (optional)

Chopped flat-leaf (Italian) parsley

1. In a medium saucepan, heat olive oil over medium heat. Add onion and garlic; cook, stirring occasionally, for 3 to 5 minutes, until onion is translucent. Add veggie ground beef; cook for 3 minutes, stirring occasionally, or until heated through.

2. Add soy milk; stir to coat the veggie ground beef. Bring to a simmer, stirring occasionally, for 3 to 5 minutes, until soy milk has evaporated. Stir in tomatoes (with juice), oregano, ½ tsp (2 mL) sea salt and a pinch of pepper. Reduce heat to medium-low, partially cover and simmer, stirring occasionally. If the sauce becomes too dry, add ½ cup (125 mL) water as necessary.

3. Meanwhile, bring a large pot of salted water to a boil. Add spaghetti and cook according to package instructions. Using a glass measuring cup, scoop out ½ cup (125 mL) pasta water and set aside. Drain pasta and return to pot.

4. Add half the sauce to the pasta, along with ¼ cup (60 mL) reserved pasta water; stir to combine. Keep adding more sauce and water, a little at a time, until the pasta is coated.

5. You now have two options: add the remaining sauce to the pasta and toss to coat or reserve what's left to pile on each portion. Top each serving with pepper, dairy-free Parmesan cheese (if using) and parsley.

Go ahead: twirl these delicious, tomato-soaked strings onto your fork and treat yo'self!

RICOTTA MAKE THESE STUFFED SHELLS!

SERVES 4

After I left for Italy (and left my marriage), I learned an important lesson I will now pass along to you. When visiting any Italian at home, they will inevitably ask you "What would you like to eat?" This is a trick question. Do not ask for a salad, sandwich or soup! What they are really asking is "Which pasta would you like?" Ricotta- and mushroom-stuffed shells in béchamel is one of my favorites.

> • **FOOD PROCESSOR**
> • **13- BY 9-INCH (33 BY 23 CM) CASSEROLE DISH**

1½ cups (375 mL) medium-firm tofu, pressed (page 15) and coarsely chopped

1 tbsp (15 mL) white miso paste

1 tsp (5 mL) garlic powder

Sea salt

1½ tbsp (22 mL) freshly squeezed lemon juice

3 tbsp (45 mL) olive oil, divided

1 tbsp (15 mL) minced garlic, divided

8 oz (250 g) cremini mushrooms, finely chopped

8 oz (250 g) large shell pasta

1 cup (250 mL) grated dairy-free Parmesan cheese or mozzarella shreds, divided

6 tbsp (90 mL) chopped fresh parsley, divided

¼ cup (60 mL) dairy-free butter

6 tbsp (90 mL) unbleached all-purpose flour

2 cups (500 mL) unsweetened soy milk

Pinch ground nutmeg

Freshly ground black pepper

1. Preheat the oven to 425°F (220°C).

2. In the food processor, combine tofu, miso paste, garlic powder, ¼ tsp (1 mL) sea salt, lemon juice and 1 tbsp (15 mL) olive oil. Process until smooth. Set aside.

3. In a medium saucepan, heat the remaining 2 tbsp (30 mL) olive oil and 2 tsp (10 mL) garlic over medium-high heat. Cook for about 2 minutes, until garlic begins to brown slightly. Add mushrooms and a pinch of sea salt; cook until mushrooms begin to brown.

4. Meanwhile, bring a large pot of salted water to a boil. Cook shells to al dente. Drain and set aside.

5. To the medium saucepan, add tofu mixture, ½ cup (125 mL) dairy-free cheese and ¼ cup (60 mL) parsley. Stir until cheese is completely melted. Set aside.

6. In a separate medium saucepan, melt dairy-free butter over medium heat. Add the remaining 1 tsp (5 mL) garlic; cook, stirring constantly, for about 2 minutes, until browned slightly. Whisk in flour and cook until thickened and a light beige paste forms.

7. Slowly add soy milk, whisking constantly, and increase heat to medium-high. Whisk in nutmeg and bring to a gentle boil. Your béchamel should begin to thicken. Remove from heat and whisk in the remaining ½ cup (125 mL) dairy-free cheese, until melted.

8. Spread a thin layer of béchamel sauce on the bottom of the casserole dish. Using a spoon, fill each shell with the mushroom mixture and arrange in an even layer in the dish. Pour the remaining béchamel over the shells.

9. Bake in the preheated oven for 15 to 20 minutes, until golden brown on top. Season with pepper.

10. Garnish with the remaining 2 tbsp (30 mL) parsley.

KRABBY PATTY

SERVES 4

Admit it, you've been searching for the secret ingredient to the Krabby Patty since childhood. I've heard that it's sand or even crab, but if I know the kindness of Mr. SquarePants, it's love. *(Plus, it'd be weird for Mr. Krabs to unalive his own kind for burgers . . . dark.)* This under the sea–inspired vegan delicacy is stacked with the bottom bun, nori aioli, patty with cheese, lettuce, onion, tomato, ketchup, mustard and three pickles. In that order.

• GRILL PAN (OPTIONAL)

½ cup (125 mL) egg-free mayo

½ tsp (2 mL) grated lemon zest

1 tsp (5 mL) ground toasted nori (see *Hack It!*)

1½ tsp (7 mL) Old Bay seasoning, divided

4 veggie burger patties

4 dairy-free Cheddar cheese slices

4 sesame seed burger buns

4 butter lettuce leaves

¼ cup (60 mL) prepared crispy onions

4 tomato slices

¼ cup (60 mL) ketchup

2 tbsp (30 mL) yellow mustard

12 dill pickle medallions

1 In a small bowl, whisk together egg-free mayo, lemon zest, nori and ½ tsp (2 mL) Old Bay seasoning. It's nori aioli! Set aside.

2 Heat the grill pan or a large skillet over medium-high heat. Evenly sprinkle both sides of each patty with the remaining 1 tsp (5 mL) Old Bay seasoning. Cook patties for 3 to 4 minutes. Flip, top each with a slice of cheese, cover and cook for another 2 to 3 minutes, until cheese has melted.

3 Meanwhile, microwave the buns on High for 15 seconds, until warm.

4 **BUILD YOUR KRABBY PATTY** Spread about 2 tbsp (30 mL) nori aioli on each bottom bun. Add veggie burger and top with 1 lettuce leaf, 1 tbsp (15 mL) crispy onions, 1 tomato slice, 1 tbsp (15 mL) ketchup, 1½ tsp (7 mL) yellow mustard, 3 pickle medallions and more aioli. In that order. Top with the other half of the bun. Serve with a side of sweet potato fries (page 183) or Brussels chips (page 187).

HACK IT!

Hey Candice! Where do I find ground toasted nori? Easy! Buy a package of toasted nori sheets from your local grocery store and grind up the sheets in a spice grinder or blender.

FOOD COURT ORANGE CAULIFLOWER

SERVES 4

Orange you glad you can make a vegan version of this sweet and tangy mall fave at home? The zesty smell of this Panda Express–inspired orange sauce always takes me back to my college days before I was of legal age to go to the bar (read: before I got fake ID) and when my girlfriends and I would hang out in the mall food court for hours between classes. Time-traveling for a quick second with each forkful of sticky cauliflower does make me grin between bites.

• RIMMED BAKING SHEET LINED WITH PARCHMENT PAPER

1 large cauliflower, cut into florets

2 tbsp (30 mL) olive oil

3 tbsp (45 mL) cornstarch, divided

2 tbsp (30 mL) grated orange zest

¼ tsp (1 mL) red pepper flakes

⅓ cup (75 mL) pure maple syrup

¼ cup (60 mL) white vinegar

¼ cup (60 mL) no-pulp orange juice

3 tbsp (45 mL) tamari or soy sauce

2 tbsp (30 mL) freshly squeezed lemon juice

1 tbsp (15 mL) toasted sesame oil

1 tbsp (15 mL) grated ginger

1 garlic clove, minced

4 cups (1 L) cooked rice

½ cup (125 mL) chopped green onion

Sesame seeds

1. Preheat the oven to 425°F (220°C).

2. In a large bowl, combine cauliflower and olive oil. Sprinkle with 2 tbsp (30 mL) cornstarch; toss to coat completely. Transfer to the prepared baking sheet.

3. Bake in the preheated oven for 15 minutes. Gently toss and bake for another 10 minutes, or until golden brown. If you want the cauliflower extra crispy, turn the oven to broil once the baking time is finished. With the oven door open, broil for 1 minute, or until you get some charred pieces. Set aside.

4. Meanwhile, prepare your orange sauce in a small bowl. Combine orange zest, the remaining 1 tbsp (15 mL) cornstarch, red pepper flakes, maple syrup, white vinegar, orange juice, tamari, lemon juice and sesame oil.

5. Heat a large skillet over high heat. Add ginger and garlic; cook for 30 seconds to 1 minute, until fragrant. Add orange sauce and bring to a boil. Boil until sauce is thick enough to coat the back of a spoon. Remove from heat. Add roasted cauliflower and stir to coat each piece thoroughly in sauce.

6. Divide rice among four plates. Top with cauliflower and sauce, and garnish with green onion and sesame seeds.

THE DIVORCED DAD'S DILL-ICIOUS VEGAN DINNER

SERVES 4

I wanted a dinner that would have everything you need to hit a peak healthy meal but was easy enough for a newly divorced dad to throw together before he got his kids for the weekend. [*Insert childhood divorce trauma here.*] It's like one of those fancy and on-trend keto bowls but cheap and made on a sheet.

> • **RIMMED BAKING SHEET LINED WITH PARCHMENT PAPER**
> • **HIGH-POWERED BLENDER**

½ cup (125 mL) quinoa, rinsed

1 cup (250 mL) water

Sea salt

1 small zucchini, cut into half-moons

1 small red onion, chopped

1 can (14 oz/398 mL) white navy beans, drained and rinsed

2 cups (500 mL) trimmed green beans

1 cup (250 mL) cherry tomatoes

¼ cup (60 mL) olive oil, divided

2 tsp (10 mL) garlic powder

1 tsp (5 mL) dried oregano

1 tsp (5 mL) dried basil

Freshly ground black pepper

3 cups (750 mL) chopped kale

DILL SAUCE

1 cup (250 mL) raw cashews, soaked (page 15), drained and rinsed

½ tsp (2 mL) onion powder

½ tsp (2 mL) garlic powder

¼ tsp (1 mL) sea salt (approx.)

½ cup (125 mL) water

2 tsp (10 mL) freshly squeezed lemon juice

1 tbsp (15 mL) dried dill

1½ tsp (7 mL) dried parsley

Freshly ground black pepper (optional)

1   Preheat the oven to 400°F (200°C).

2   In a medium saucepan, combine quinoa, water and a pinch of sea salt; bring to a boil. Reduce heat to low, cover and cook for 15 minutes. Let stand for 5 minutes, then fluff with a fork.

3   Meanwhile, on the prepared baking sheet, add zucchini, onion, navy beans, green beans and tomatoes. Drizzle 3 tbsp (45 mL) olive oil over top; toss to coat. Sprinkle with garlic powder, oregano, basil, ¼ tsp (1 mL) sea salt and ¼ tsp (1 mL) pepper. Toss with your hands and spread veggies out evenly on the baking sheet.

4   Bake in the preheated oven for 20 to 25 minutes, tossing halfway, until veggies are browned slightly.

5   Meanwhile, in a medium bowl, toss kale with the remaining 1 tbsp (15 mL) olive oil and massage until bright green. Add kale to the baking sheet with the roasting veggies when you have 5 to 8 minutes left of cooking time. Cook until kale is charred.

6   **DILL SAUCE** In the high-powered blender, combine cashews, onion powder, garlic powder, sea salt, water and lemon juice; blend on high speed until smooth. Transfer to a small bowl and stir in dill and parsley. Season to taste with sea salt and pepper.

7   In a large bowl, combine cooked quinoa and roasted veggies, along with any liquid from the baking sheet. Gently toss to mix. Season to taste with sea salt and pepper, if desired.

8   Serve hot, drizzled with dill sauce and extra sauce on the side.

HACK IT!

Want more protein? Just toss in your favorite cooked plant-based meat substitute, like sliced plant-based sausage, marinated tofu or sliced veggie nuggets, in Step 7.

EASY BREEZY CREAMY CHIC-PEAS

SERVES 4

Do not underestimate the power of a one-pan meal after a busy workday, especially when there's leftover rice in the fridge. Aromatic, creamy and comforting, this 10-minute dinner turns chickpeas into tomato-and-herb-soaked chic-peas. You're about to kill it with this skillet!

2 tbsp (30 mL) olive oil

4 garlic cloves, thinly sliced

2 large shallots, thinly sliced

1 tsp (5 mL) dried thyme

¼ tsp (1 mL) red pepper flakes

Sea salt

2 tbsp (30 mL) capers, drained

1 can (28 oz/796 mL) chickpeas, drained

2 tsp (10 mL) paprika

1 tbsp (15 mL) tomato paste

2 cups (500 mL) full-fat coconut milk

Freshly ground black pepper

2 tbsp (30 mL) chopped fresh parsley

4 cups (1 L) cooked brown rice, warm

4 gluten-free flatbread, pita or naan (optional)

1 In a large skillet, heat olive oil over medium-high heat. Add garlic, shallots, thyme, red pepper flakes and a pinch of sea salt; cook for 1 to 2 minutes, until garlic is lightly golden. Add capers and cook for 1 minute.

2 Add chickpeas, coconut milk, tomato paste and paprika; bring to a boil, stirring frequently. Reduce heat to medium and simmer for 5 minutes, or until thickened slightly. Season to taste with sea salt and pepper.

3 Remove from heat and sprinkle parsley over top. Serve with brown rice and flatbread (if using).

HACK IT!

Bulk up this recipe by adding your favorite cooked plant-based protein in Step 2. I love including some plant-based chicken substitute, smoked tofu cubes, tofu ricotta or even Mixed Herb and Garlic Chèvre (page 111).

MAKE YOU HORNO PASTA AL FORNO

SERVES 4

Just call me Candice Carb-dashian, because these noods are gonna make me famous! (Or infamous if any of my Italian friends find out I condone one-pot pasta.) Don't get me wrong, I too would normally put on my I've-been-to-Italy-and-so-I-could-never-eat-one-pot-pasta pants, but I am also a vegan witch who can make almost anything work. And this creamy, veggie-packed and cheese-baked pasta of your dreams is the only noods dish I'm sending these days.

1 tbsp (15 mL) olive oil

½ medium onion, chopped

3 garlic cloves, minced

½ lb (250 g) plant-based chicken strips, cut into bite-sized chunks

Sea salt

3 cups (750 mL) rotini pasta

½ cube (½ tsp/2 mL) no-chicken or vegetable bouillon

1 cup (250 mL) water

1½ cups (375 mL) unsweetened soy milk

1½ cups (375 mL) small broccoli florets

¾ cup (175 mL) frozen peas

2 cups (500 mL) dairy-free Cheddar cheese shreds, divided

Pinch ground nutmeg

Freshly ground black pepper

2 tbsp (30 mL) chopped flat-leaf (Italian) parsley

1   Preheat the oven to 450°F (230°C).

2   In a large oven-safe skillet, heat olive oil over medium-high heat. Add onion, garlic, plant-based chicken strips and a pinch of sea salt; cook, stirring occasionally, for 3 to 5 minutes, until onion is translucent and the plant-based chicken strips are slightly browned and heated through.

3   Add pasta, bouillon, soy milk and water; bring to a boil, stirring frequently. Reduce heat to medium-low, cover and simmer for 10 to 12 minutes, stirring occasionally, until pasta is cooked.

4   Stir in broccoli, peas, 1 cup (250 mL) dairy-free cheese shreds and nutmeg; cook, uncovered, for about 3 minutes, until the sauce has reduced slightly and peas are heated through. Season to taste with sea salt and pepper. Top with the remaining 1 cup (250 mL) dairy-free cheese shreds.

5   Bake in the preheated oven for 3 to 5 minutes, until cheese has melted.

6   Remove from the oven and garnish with parsley; serve.

THE GOOEY MESSY LENTIL BURGER AKA SLOPPY JOE

SERVES 4 TO 6

My dad used to make us sloppy joes and, in totally unconventional parent fashion, would host a "messiest eater" contest. (*Tell me you had a single dad without telling me you had a single dad.*) He took "I made 'em extra slopppppy for ya!" literally. These days, I refrain from smearing meaty tomato sauce all over my face, but if I'm feeling fancy, I call it a sloppy Giuseppe.

1 tbsp (15 mL) olive oil

1 small onion, finely chopped

½ red bell pepper, finely chopped

2 garlic cloves, minced

½ cup (125 mL) dried brown lentils, rinsed

1 tsp (5 mL) ground cumin

½ tsp (2 mL) chili powder

½ tsp (2 mL) paprika

2⅓ cups (575 mL) water (approx.), divided

1 tbsp (15 mL) cornstarch

1 cup (250 mL) veggie ground beef

1 can (14 oz/398 mL) crushed tomatoes (with juice)

¼ cup (60 mL) vegan-friendly BBQ sauce

1 tbsp (15 mL) vegan Worcestershire sauce

Sea salt and freshly ground black pepper

4 tsp to 2 tbsp (20 to 30 mL) dairy-free butter

4 to 6 hamburger buns, toasted

OPTIONAL TOPPINGS

Pickled onions or dill pickle medallions

Hot sauce

Sliced jalapeño peppers

Prepared coleslaw or Pineapple Slaw (see opposite)

Mustard and/or vegan-friendly BBQ sauce

1   In a large saucepan, heat olive oil over medium-high heat. Add onion, red pepper and garlic; cook, stirring occasionally, for 3 to 5 minutes, until onion is translucent.

2   Add lentils, cumin, chili powder, paprika and 2 cups (500 mL) water. Bring to a boil, stirring frequently. Reduce heat to medium and cook, stirring occasionally, for 15 minutes.

3   Cover and simmer for another 15 minutes, or until lentils are tender. Add more water ¼ cup (60 mL) at a time if the lentils are dry.

4   Meanwhile, in a small bowl, whisk together cornstarch and the remaining 1 tbsp (15 mL) water. Set aside.

5   To the saucepan, stir in veggie ground beef, crushed tomatoes (with juice), BBQ sauce, vegan Worcestershire and cornstarch mixture; bring to a boil over medium-high heat. Reduce heat to medium, cover and simmer for 5 to 10 minutes, stirring occasionally, until heated through. Season to taste with sea salt and pepper.

6   Spread 1 tsp (5 mL) dairy-free butter on each bottom bun. Pile lentils high onto each bottom bun and garnish with any of the toppings you desire, followed by the bun top.

JERK-SEASONED CHICKPEA TACOS WITH PINEAPPLE SLAW

SERVES 4

I love Caribbean food and, more specifically, anything jerk. It's a distinctly bold, spicy and fresh flavor that 100% influenced these perfectly hog-worthy chickpea tacos. Topped with a creamy aioli and pineapple slaw and served in a warm tortilla, this dish is quick enough to make on a weeknight and impressive enough to serve to friends.

PINEAPPLE SLAW

1 tbsp (15 mL) olive oil

1 tbsp (15 mL) freshly squeezed lime juice

2 cups (500 mL) chopped pineapple

2 cups (500 mL) shredded green or red cabbage (or both!)

¼ small red onion, finely chopped

¼ cup (60 mL) fresh cilantro, chopped

Sea salt

JERK AIOLI

1 cup (250 mL) egg-free mayo

1 tbsp (15 mL) freshly squeezed lime juice

1 to 2 tsp (5 to 10 mL) hot sauce (optional)

2 tsp (10 mL) jerk seasoning

CHICKPEA TACOS

2 garlic cloves, minced

2 tbsp (30 mL) jerk seasoning

2 tbsp (30 mL) olive oil

1 tbsp (15 mL) freshly squeezed lime juice

1 tbsp (15 mL) tamari or soy sauce

3 cups (750 mL) chickpeas, drained and rinsed

12 small corn or flour tortillas

1 **PINEAPPLE SLAW** In a medium bowl, whisk together olive oil and lime juice. Add pineapple, cabbage, onion and cilantro; toss to coat. Season to taste with sea salt. Set aside.

2 **JERK AIOLI** In a small bowl, whisk together egg-free mayo, lime juice, hot sauce (if using) and jerk seasoning. Set aside.

3 **CHICKPEA TACOS** In a separate medium bowl, whisk together garlic, jerk seasoning, olive oil, lime juice and tamari. Add chickpeas; toss to coat in the marinade.

4 Heat a medium skillet over medium-high heat. Once hot, add chickpeas and marinade; cook for about 5 minutes, until the chickpeas are heated through.

5 Wrap tortillas in a clean dish towel and microwave on High in 15-second intervals until warm.

6 Divide chickpeas among 12 tortillas. Top with pineapple slaw and a drizzle of jerk aioli; serve.

HACK IT!

You can make this recipe with almost any plant-based protein you love. Try it with seitan, soy curls, black or pinto beans, mushrooms or cooked lentils.

The jerk aioli keeps in the fridge for up to 5 days and makes an awesome dipping sauce or sandwich spread. The taco filling and pineapple slaw will keep in the fridge for up to 3 days. Try the slaw on its own as a fresh salad, or to top a sandwich.

MUSHROOM FAJITAS THAT GIVE A SHEET

SERVES 4

You know when someone orders fajitas at a restaurant and they come to the table sizzling on a skillet, demanding the eyes of everyone in the room? These aren't that. These are tasty fajitas on the down-low. They know their worth in flavor and they don't need to be loud about it — they aren't overcompensating for anything.

- **BAKING SHEET LINED WITH PARCHMENT PAPER**
- **HIGH-POWERED BLENDER**

MUSHROOM FAJITAS

1½ tsp (7 mL) ground cumin

1 tsp (5 mL) chili powder

1 tsp (5 mL) paprika

1 tsp (5 mL) garlic powder

1 tsp (5 mL) dried oregano

¼ cup (60 mL) olive oil

6 large portobello mushrooms, sliced

1 red bell pepper, cut into ½-inch (1 cm) slices

1 yellow bell pepper, cut into ½-inch (1 cm) slices

1 green bell pepper, cut into ½-inch (1 cm) slices

1 medium onion, sliced

Sea salt and freshly ground black pepper

12 small corn or flour tortillas

¼ cup (60 mL) fresh cilantro, chopped

CHILI-LIME CREMA

1 cup (250 mL) raw cashews, soaked (page 15)

¼ to ½ cup (60 to 125 mL) chopped green chiles (depending on heat tolerance)

1 tsp (5 mL) garlic powder

Sea salt

½ cup (125 mL) water

2 tbsp (30 mL) freshly squeezed lime juice

1. **MUSHROOM FAJITAS** Preheat the oven to 400°F (200°C).

2. On the prepared baking sheet, pile up cumin, chili powder, paprika, garlic powder and oregano. Add olive oil and give it a swirl with your finger to combine.

3. To the baking sheet, add mushrooms, red pepper, yellow pepper, green pepper and onion. Toss with the spiced olive oil mixture to coat. Spread out veggies in a single layer and sprinkle with sea salt and pepper.

4. Bake in the preheated oven for 15 minutes. Remove veggies from the oven, stir, then bake for another 5 minutes, or until lightly browned.

5. Meanwhile, wrap tortillas in foil and warm in the oven for the final 5 minutes the veggies are roasting.

6. **CHILI-LIME CREMA** Meanwhile, drain and rinse cashews. In the high-powered blender, add cashews, green chiles, garlic powder, ½ tsp (2 mL) sea salt, water and lime juice; blend on high speed until smooth. Season to taste with sea salt. Set aside.

7. Remove the veggies from the oven and season to taste with sea salt, if desired. Sprinkle with cilantro; toss to mix.

8. Serve with optional toppings on the side (see *Hack It!*). Let everyone add roasted veggies and toppings to their tortillas as desired.

HACK IT!

Add more protein to this dish by simply tossing in some tofu cubes, seitan slices or prepared veggie meat of choice in Step 3.

Optional toppings: shredded lettuce, mashed ripe avocado, tomato salsa, refried beans and dairy-free sour cream

LIGHTNING-FAST MINI MEATLOAVES

SERVES 4

Meatloaf! A dinner so classic and filled with ketchup it falls somewhere between a fifties housewife and a seventies "Bat Out of Hell" rock star. These juicy cuties are easy to make ahead, cook in half the time of regular-sized meatloaf and make for great leftovers. Once you see the extra surface area slathered with that coveted sticky glaze, you'll wonder why you didn't make them teeny sooner.

• 11- BY 7-INCH (28 BY 18 CM) CASSEROLE DISH LINED WITH PARCHMENT PAPER

1 large carrot, grated

½ small onion, diced

1 lb (500 g) veggie ground beef

1 cup (250 mL) dried bread crumbs

1 cup (250 mL) coarsely chopped cremini mushrooms

1 tsp (5 mL) Italian seasoning

½ tsp (2 mL) garlic powder

¼ tsp (1 mL) freshly ground black pepper

Sea salt

1 prepared vegan egg (see *Hack It!*)

½ cup (125 mL) ketchup, divided

1 tbsp (15 mL) soy sauce

2 tbsp (30 mL) pure maple syrup

1 tsp (5 mL) yellow mustard

1   Preheat the oven to 400°F (200°C).

2   In a large bowl, using your hands, combine carrot, onion, veggie ground beef, bread crumbs, mushrooms, Italian seasoning, garlic powder, pepper, a pinch of sea salt, vegan egg, ¼ cup (60 mL) ketchup and soy sauce.

3   In a small bowl, whisk together the remaining ¼ cup (60 mL) ketchup, maple syrup and yellow mustard. Set aside.

4   Using your hands, form four even-sized little loaves and place in the prepared casserole dish. Brush with half the ketchup glaze.

5   Bake in the preheated oven for 15 minutes. Remove from the oven and brush with the remaining glaze. Bake for another 5 minutes, or until glaze is sticky.

6   Remove from the oven and let stand for 10 minutes to cool slightly. Store leftovers in an airtight container in the fridge for up to 5 days.

HACK IT!

Vegan egg replacers are readily available, premixed combinations of starches and leavening agents that can be used in recipes calling for eggs as a binding agent. Follow the package instructions to make the equivalent of 1 egg for this recipe.

CRUNCHY CHALUPA TACOS

SERVES 4

These days, the only fitness I'm doing is fit'ness Taco Bell–inspired "beefy chalupa" in my mouth. Exercise is hard. And I am much more inclined to do it if it comes with a tasty reward. But on the rare occasion I do deign to lift a thing and put it down repeatedly, for no good reason, you can bet your ass I'll be indulging in this beefed-up fried naan taco drizzled with avocado-ranch immediately afterward.

- **DEEP FRYER OR HEAVY-BOTTOMED SAUCEPAN FITTED WITH A DEEP-FRY THERMOMETER**
- **WIRE RACK OVER A RIMMED BAKING SHEET**

AVOCADO-RANCH SAUCE

½ ripe avocado, mashed

¼ **cup (60 mL)** dairy-free sour cream

¼ **cup (60 mL)** egg-free mayo

2 tsp (10 mL) onion powder

1 tsp (5 mL) garlic powder

1 tsp (5 mL) dried parsley

1 tsp (5 mL) dried dill

1 tbsp (15 mL) unsweetened non-dairy milk

1½ **tsp (7 mL)** white vinegar

TACOS

Vegetable oil

1 lb (500 g) veggie ground beef

¼ **cup (60 mL)** unbleached all-purpose flour

1 package (1 oz/30 g) taco seasoning

1 cup (250 mL) water

4 naan

1 cup (250 mL) shredded lettuce

½ **cup (125 mL)** dairy-free Cheddar cheese shreds

¼ **cup (60 mL)** diced tomato

1 **AVOCADO-RANCH SAUCE** In a small bowl, combine avocado, dairy-free sour cream, egg-free mayo, onion powder, garlic powder, parsley, dill, non-dairy milk and white vinegar until smooth. Place in the fridge while you prepare the rest of the recipe. *Mmm . . . avocado-ranch sauce.*

2 **TACOS** In the deep fryer or a heavy-bottomed saucepan, heat vegetable oil to 375°F (190°C). If you're frying on the stovetop, you'll need at least 3 inches (7.5 cm) oil.

3 Meanwhile, heat a large skillet over medium-high heat. Combine veggie ground beef, flour, taco seasoning and water; bring to a boil. Reduce heat to medium-low and simmer for 3 to 5 minutes, until liquid has reduced by half. Keep warm over low heat.

4 Meanwhile, using tongs, deep-fry naan one at a time for about 15 seconds, until soft. Remove from oil and immediately fold naan in half using the tongs — it should look like a taco. Return to hot oil and fry for 30 seconds to 1 minute, until golden and crunchy. Transfer shells to the prepared wire rack to allow excess oil to drip off. Let oil return to 375°F (190°C) between batches.

5 To fill your chalupas, layer veggie ground beef mixture, avocado-ranch sauce, lettuce, dairy-free cheese and tomatoes in the fried naan. Don't forget the extra avo-ranch on the side for dipping!

MASSAMAN-STYLE TOFU CURRY

SERVES 4

Thai cuisine is absolute perfection — and despite being on my travel bucket list for the last 10 years, I *still* haven't made it to Thailand. For now, I'll keep dreaming of a beach vacation and this homemade animal-friendly version of massaman curry. It's super satisfying and complex yet surprisingly easy to make at home with a few shortcuts from the traditional recipe.

2 tbsp (30 mL) coconut oil

1 medium onion, chopped

4 garlic cloves, minced

1 tbsp (15 mL) grated gingerroot

1 tsp (5 mL) ground cumin

1 tsp (5 mL) ground turmeric

¼ cup (60 mL) massaman or red curry paste

1½ tsp (7 mL) tamarind paste

1 package (16 oz/450 g) extra-firm tofu, pressed (page 15) and cubed

1 tbsp (15 mL) tamari or soy sauce

1 tsp (5 mL) grated lemon zest

Sea salt

2 yellow potatoes, peeled and cubed

2 star anise pods

1 cinnamon stick

½ cup (125 mL) roasted peanuts

1 cup (250 mL) water

1 can (14 oz/398 mL) full-fat coconut milk

3 tbsp (45 mL) creamy peanut butter

1 tbsp (15 mL) brown sugar

1 tbsp (15 mL) freshly squeezed lime juice

4 cups (1 L) cooked rice of choice (optional)

Chopped cilantro

1   In a large saucepan or wok, heat coconut oil over medium heat. Add onion, garlic, ginger, cumin and turmeric; cook, stirring occasionally, for 3 to 5 minutes, until onion is translucent.

2   Stir in massaman curry paste, tamarind paste, tofu, tamari, lemon zest and 1 tsp (5 mL) sea salt. Cook for about 3 minutes, until tofu is heated through.

3   Add potatoes, star anise, cinnamon stick, peanuts and water; bring to a boil. Reduce heat to medium; add coconut milk and peanut butter; stir. Simmer for about 15 minutes, until potatoes are fork-tender.

4   Stir in brown sugar and lime juice. Season to taste with sea salt and serve with rice (if using). Garnish with cilantro.

HACK IT!

Try this recipe using your favorite plant-based chicken or beef instead of tofu.

I'M DRUNK! NOODLES!

SERVES 2

You'll be okay, we've all been there. You just need to get yourself a glass of water and ask the party-mom friend in the group to whip up these noodles. A slice of pizza at the end of the night is fine, but what's really going to satisfy those post-bar cravings (and not sit too heavy in your tummy full of tequila) is a bowl of veggies and noodles in a sweet and slightly spicy sauce.

4 oz (125 g) vermicelli rice noodles

1 tsp (5 mL) vegetable oil

2 garlic cloves, minced

3 tbsp (45 mL) soy sauce

2 tsp (10 mL) sambal oelek

1 tsp (5 mL) brown sugar or pure maple syrup

1 cup (250 mL) packed bean sprouts

½ cup (125 mL) frozen peas

1 tsp (5 mL) toasted sesame oil

1 green onion, green parts only, thinly sliced

Sesame seeds (optional)

1   Cook noodles according to package instructions. Set aside.

2   In a large skillet or wok, heat vegetable oil over medium-high heat. Add garlic and cook for about 1 minute, until fragrant.

3   Add soy sauce, sambal oelek and brown sugar; cook, stirring constantly, until sugar dissolves. Add bean sprouts and peas; cook for 2 to 3 minutes, until heated through. Add cooked noodles and sesame oil; toss to coat noodles completely in sauce.

4   Garnish with green onion and a sprinkle of sesame seeds (if using). Enjoy!

HACK IT!

Want less washing up? Cut your green onion with scissors! *You shouldn't be using a knife in your state anyway . . .*

GNOCCHI SAUSAGE FEST

SERVES 4

You put your onions in, you take your sausage out. You pour tomatoes in and you shake the spinach all about. You do the hokey gnocchi and you get yourself some cheese. A quick dinner's what it's all about it! Hey!

2 tbsp (30 mL) olive oil

1 small onion, chopped

3 garlic cloves, minced

1 lb (500 g) plant-based Italian sausage, crumbled

1 can (14 oz/398 mL) diced tomatoes (with juice)

¼ cup (60 mL) vegetable broth

2 packages (each 16 oz/450 g) prepared potato gnocchi

3 cups (750 mL) fresh spinach

Sea salt and freshly ground black pepper

½ cup (125 mL) grated dairy-free Parmesan or mozzarella shreds (optional)

1. In a large skillet, heat olive oil over medium-high heat. Add onion and garlic; cook, stirring occasionally, for 3 to 5 minutes, until onion is translucent.

2. Add plant-based sausage and cook for 2 minutes, or until slightly browned. Stir in tomatoes (with juice), vegetable broth and gnocchi. Reduce heat to medium, cover and cook for 5 minutes, or until gnocchi is tender.

3. Remove the skillet from the heat and stir in spinach. Cover and cook for 1 minute, or until wilted. Season to taste with sea salt and pepper.

4. Remove from heat. Sprinkle with dairy-free Parmesan cheese (if using) and cover for 1 minute, or until cheese has melted.

5. Divide among four bowls and serve with sliced Italian crusty bread to sop up any leftover sauce.

Looking for a gluten-free snack?
Spoon some egg salad onto a lettuce
leaf, wrap it up and enjoy!

OFFICE-APPROPRIATE TOFU-EGG SALAD SANDWICHES

SERVES 4

Back when I worked for The Man, I was on a pretty tight budget. I tried to bring my lunch every day. Although I loved the humble egg salad sandwich, I never dared to pack it because I'd seen the shame that comes with opening a container of hard-boiled eggs in a densely populated lunchroom (*Ewwww, David!*). Luckily for all of us, this tofu-based egg salad sandwich is happily pungent-free!

1 tbsp (15 mL) nutritional yeast

½ tsp (2 mL) garlic powder

Kala namak or sea salt

¼ tsp (1 mL) ground turmeric

¼ tsp (1 mL) paprika

Freshly ground black pepper

⅓ cup (75 mL) egg-free mayo

1 tbsp (15 mL) apple cider vinegar

2 tsp (10 mL) Dijon mustard

2 tsp (10 mL) sweet relish

1 package (16 oz/450 g) medium-firm tofu, pressed (page 15) and crumbled

1 stalk celery, finely chopped

½ small red onion, finely chopped

1 tbsp (15 mL) chopped fresh parsley

1 tbsp (15 mL) finely chopped fresh dill or chives (optional)

8 sandwich bread slices

8 green leaf lettuce leaves

1 tomato, sliced

1 cup (250 mL) alfalfa, radish or sunflower sprouts of choice

Sea salt

1   In a large bowl, combine nutritional yeast, garlic powder, ½ tsp (2 mL) kala namak, turmeric, paprika, ¼ tsp (1 mL) pepper, egg-free mayo, apple cider vinegar, Dijon and relish until smooth.

2   To the large bowl, add tofu, celery, onion, parsley and dill (if using). Stir gently to combine and season to taste with kala namak and pepper. You can use this egg salad right away on its own in a sandwich or chill in the fridge for up to 3 days to allow the flavors to meld.

3   **TO BUILD YOUR SANDWICH** First decide if you're feeling toasty or not today! If so, toast some bread. Place 2 pieces of lettuce on 4 bread slices. Add tomato, tofu mixture, sprouts and a sprinkle of sea salt. Top with a second slice of bread. Slice sandwich in half and serve or wrap it up for a delicious school or work lunch.

HACK IT!

Try this egg salad on an avocado toast, topped with 1 to 2 tbsp (15 to 30 mL) pickled onion. It's a to-die-for brunch!

ESSENCE OF THE SEA PO'BOY

SERVES 4

Transport yourself to New Orleans with marinated and breaded hearts of palm "oysters," fried to golden perfection, served on a bun and topped with a creamy rémoulade. But proceed with caution and consider protective eyewear, 'cause whomever you're serving may just start throwing Mardi Gras beads at you in celebration.

> • **DEEP FRYER OR HEAVY-BOTTOMED SAUCEPAN FITTED WITH A DEEP-FRY THERMOMETER**

2 garlic cloves, minced

2 tbsp (30 mL) ground toasted nori (see *Hack It!* page 138)

2 tsp (10 mL) Old Bay seasoning, divided

¼ cup (60 mL) soy sauce

¼ cup (60 mL) olive oil

2 tbsp (30 mL) freshly squeezed lime juice

1 can (14 oz/398 mL) hearts of palm, drained and sliced

1 tbsp (15 mL) minced celery

½ tsp (2 mL) minced capers

2 tsp (10 mL) Creole seasoning

½ cup (125 mL) egg-free mayo

1 tbsp (15 mL) Dijon mustard

1 tbsp (15 mL) freshly squeezed lemon juice

5 tsp (25 mL) hot sauce (approx.), divided

½ cup (125 mL) unsweetened soy milk

1½ tsp (7 mL) white vinegar

½ cup (125 mL) unbleached all-purpose flour, divided

3 tbsp (45 mL) cornmeal

1 tsp (5 mL) baking powder

¼ tsp (1 mL) sea salt

Vegetable oil

4 French or hoagie rolls, split

1¼ cups (310 mL) shredded iceberg lettuce

2 tomatoes, sliced

16 pickle medallions

1. In a medium bowl, whisk together garlic, nori, 1 tsp (5 mL) Old Bay seasoning, soy sauce, olive oil and lime juice. Add hearts of palm; gently toss to coat completely. Let stand for 15 minutes.

2. Meanwhile, in a small bowl, stir together celery, capers, Creole seasoning, egg-free mayo, Dijon, lemon juice and 2 tsp (10 mL) hot sauce. You've got a rémoulade! Put in the fridge while you prepare the rest of the recipe.

3. In a separate small bowl, whisk together soy milk and white vinegar. Set aside.

4. In a large bowl, whisk together ¼ cup (60 mL) flour, cornmeal, baking powder, sea salt, the remaining 1 tsp (5 mL) Old Bay seasoning and 1 tbsp (15 mL) hot sauce. Slowly whisk in soy milk mixture until the batter is smooth. Let stand for 15 minutes.

5. In a large shallow bowl, add the remaining ¼ cup (60 mL) flour.

6. Meanwhile, in the deep fryer or a heavy-bottomed saucepan, heat vegetable oil to 375°F (190°C). If you're frying on the stove, you'll need at least 1 inch (2.5 cm) oil.

7. Working in batches, dip hearts of palm into the batter, then toss to coat in flour, shaking off excess flour.

8. Fry hearts of palm in the hot oil for 2 to 3 minutes, until golden brown and crispy. Place on a wire rack to help them retain their crispiness.

9. Now it's time to build your sandwich! Spread the bottom half of each roll with rémoulade, then top with about ⅓ cup (75 mL) lettuce, tomato slices, 4 pickles, and loads of fried hearts of palm and hot sauce (if using). Serve.

SWEDISH MEATBALLS

SERVES 4 TO 6

I know the Swedish Chef personally, and he wanted me to tell you that these vegan meatballs are the perfect thing to eat between drinking brännvin and assembling an Ikea bedside table. They are swimming in a delectably rich brown sauce that is as easy to drink (at least, I think so) as it is to make. No Allen key required.

¼ **cup (60 mL)** olive oil, divided

2 lbs (1 kg) plant-based meatballs (see *Hack It!*)

2 cubes (each 1 tsp/5 mL) no-beef or vegetable bouillon

3 cups (750 mL) water

1 tsp (5 mL) mushroom seasoning or 2 tbsp (30 mL) soy sauce (see *Hack It!*)

2 tbsp (30 mL) Dijon mustard

⅓ **cup (75 mL)** dairy-free butter or margarine

¾ **cup (175 mL)** unbleached all-purpose flour

½ **cup (125 mL)** unsweetened soy milk

Sea salt and freshly ground black pepper

3 tbsp (45 mL) chopped fresh parsley

OPTIONAL BASES

Mashed potatoes

Cooked pasta

1   In a large skillet, heat 2 tbsp (30 mL) olive oil over medium heat. Add plant-based meatballs, stirring occasionally, for 4 to 5 minutes, until browned. Transfer to a plate (reserving skillet).

2   Meanwhile, in a medium bowl, dissolve bouillon in water. Add mushroom seasoning and Dijon. Set aside.

3   In the reserved skillet, heat dairy-free butter and the remaining 2 tbsp (30 mL) olive oil over medium heat. Once butter is melted, add flour; cook, whisking constantly, for 4 to 5 minutes, until thickened and brown. Slowly whisk in bouillon mixture and then soy milk. Bring to a boil over high heat, whisking constantly, until thickened.

4   Reduce heat to medium and add meatballs. Stir to coat each meatball completely. Season to taste with sea salt and pepper.

5   Serve garnished with parsley and overtop mashed potatoes or cooked pasta (if using).

HACK IT!

I make my own meatballs by combining 2 lbs (1 kg) Beyond Meat or Impossible Foods ground meat and 3 tbsp (45 mL) dried bread crumbs in a large bowl, then roll this mixture into golf-ball-sized balls.

Mushroom seasoning can be found in the international food section of your grocery store and at your local Asian grocer.

AWESOME AUSSIE MEAT PIES

SERVES 6

There are a few questionable ways to consume these mini beefy Australian pies. The least maniacal involves removing the top of the flakey pastry, squirting some ketchup into the veggie meat and gravy, putting the top back on and biting into it. That's good as lunch in the arvo, but pair them with some creamed spinach (page 199) or roasted zucchini (page 191) and you've got yourself a righto dinner, mate! Just don't forget the ketchup.

• 6-CUP MUFFIN TIN, GREASED

1 tbsp (15 mL) olive oil

1 onion, finely chopped

1 garlic clove, minced

1 lb (500 g) veggie ground beef

2 cubes (each 1 tsp/5 mL) no-beef or vegetable bouillon

1 bay leaf

¼ tsp (1 mL) dried rosemary

¼ tsp (1 mL) sea salt

Freshly ground black pepper

1 cup (250 mL) water, divided

¼ cup (60 mL) tomato sauce

1 tbsp (15 mL) vegemite (optional)

2 tsp (10 mL) plant-based Worcestershire sauce

3 tbsp (45 mL) unbleached all-purpose flour

Two 9-inch (23 cm) prepared frozen vegan-friendly pie crusts, thawed

2 sheets (each 10 by 10 inches/ 25 by 25 cm) puff pastry dough, thawed if frozen

2 tbsp (30 mL) unsweetened soy milk

1 tbsp (15 mL) pure maple syrup

Ketchup

1 Preheat the oven to 375°F (190°C).

2 In a medium saucepan, heat olive oil over medium-high heat. Add onion and garlic; cook, stirring occasionally, for 3 to 5 minutes, until onion is translucent. Add veggie ground beef; cook for 2 minutes, or until warmed. Add bouillon, bay leaf, rosemary, sea salt, a pinch of pepper, ¾ cup (175 mL) water, tomato sauce, vegemite (if using) and plant-based Worcestershire; bring to a boil. Reduce heat to medium-low, cover and simmer for 15 minutes, stirring frequently, or until flavors have melded.

3 Stir in flour and the remaining ¼ cup (60 mL) water, and bring to a boil. Reduce heat to medium and simmer for 5 minutes, or until thickened slightly. Remove bay leaf.

4 Meanwhile, carefully transfer pie crusts to a work surface. Using the mouth of a large jar, small bowl or large glass with a 4- to 4½-inch (10 to 11 cm) diameter, cut out six circles in the pie crust. Press gently into muffins cups, leaving about a ¼-inch (0.5 cm) overhang.

5 Using the mouth of a smaller jar, bowl or glass roughly 3 inches (7.5 cm) in diameter, cut out six circles in the puff pastry.

6 Fill crust-filled muffin cups three-quarters full with beefy gravy mixture.

7 Place a 3-inch (7.5 cm) puff pastry round over each cup and press the edges into the pie crust with your fingers to create a seal. Trim excess pastry with a sharp knife.

8 In a small bowl, whisk together soy milk and maple syrup. Evenly brush tops of each pie with soy milk mixture and pierce each three to four times with a knife.

9 Bake in the preheated oven for 15 to 20 minutes, until the tops are golden. Serve with ketchup and eat as directed in my headnote — it's the only acceptable way.

HACK IT!

Fun fact! To cut costs, some baking brands use oil instead of butter in their puff pastries and pie tarts, making them incidentally vegan. Hooray for us!

LINGUINE AGLIO E OLIO

SERVES 4

Hey betch, I know you've had a rough day, so I made you this 20-minute, grown-up version of garlic buttered noodles. Keep the ingredient staples in your pantry for whenever you're hungry for a classic Italian pasta but short on time — or come home to an empty fridge.

1 lb (500 g) linguine

½ cup (125 mL) olive oil

6 garlic cloves, thinly sliced

1 tsp (5 mL) red pepper flakes

⅓ cup (75 mL) chopped fresh parsley, divided

½ to 1 cup (125 to 250 mL) dairy-free white cheese of choice

Lemon wedges

1 Bring a large pot of salted water to a boil. Add pasta and cook until al dente. Using a glass measuring cup, scoop out ½ cup (125 mL) pasta water and set aside. DO NOT DRAIN PASTA!

2 Meanwhile, in a large skillet, heat olive oil over medium heat. Add garlic; cook for 3 to 5 minutes, stirring constantly, until golden. Add red pepper flakes and cook for 1 minute.

3 Using a pasta ladle or tongs, transfer pasta from the cooking water directly into the pan with oil. Toss to coat.

4 Add reserved pasta water and ¼ cup (60 mL) parsley; toss to coat. Bring to a boil, stirring for 1 minute, or until the sauce is thick and velvety.

5 Remove from heat and stir in dairy-free white cheese until melted. Top with the remaining 1 tbsp (15 mL) parsley and serve with lemon wedges alongside each bowl.

THE ROCHESTER GARBAGE PLATE

SERVES 4

The word "garbage" here refers to the "throw it in a pile" nature of this dish. A base of French fries and macaroni salad is topped with a cheeseburger patty, then smothered with Rochester hot sauce. It's hangover food . . . on steroids — and we have the wonderful people of Nick Tahou Hots in Rochester, New York, to thank for inventing it. Sorry, Oscar, there is no actual garbage involved.

1 package (1 lb/500 g) frozen French fries

2 tbsp (30 mL) olive oil

1½ cups (375 mL) veggie ground beef

2 tsp (10 mL) paprika

1½ tsp (7 mL) brown sugar

½ tsp (2 mL) garlic powder

½ tsp (2 mL) onion powder

½ tsp (2 mL) ground cumin

Sea salt and freshly ground black pepper

¼ cup (60 mL) tomato paste

Yellow mustard

2 cubes (each 1 tsp/5 mL) no-beef or vegetable bouillon

2 cups (500 mL) water

4 veggie burger patties

4 dairy-free Cheddar cheese slices

4 cups (1 L) New York Deli Mac Salad (page 70) or prepared macaroni salad

¼ cup (60 mL) diced white onion

Ketchup

4 white bread slices, buttered

1 Prepare French fries according to package instructions.

2 Meanwhile, heat a medium saucepan over medium-high heat. Add olive oil, veggie ground beef, paprika, brown sugar, garlic powder, onion powder, cumin, ½ tsp (2 mL) pepper and ¼ tsp (1 mL) sea salt, tomato paste, 1 tbsp (15 mL) yellow mustard, bouillon and water; bring to a boil. Reduce heat to medium, cover and simmer for 15 to 20 minutes, until thickened slightly. Season to taste with sea salt and pepper.

3 Meanwhile, cook patties according to package instructions. Top each patty with a slice of dairy-free Cheddar cheese, then cover the pan with a lid to melt.

4 To build your garbage plates, evenly distribute fries onto one side of each plate and place 1 cup (250 mL) macaroni salad on the other side. Top with 1 cheesy burger patty, 1 tbsp (15 mL) onion and as much veggie ground beef sauce as each person desires. Drizzle with ketchup and yellow mustard and serve with a slice of buttered bread.

HOT POT PIE SIMMER

SERVES 4 TO 6

Soup and crackers? Hunny, I am all about that soup and pastry! This one-pot wonder has got it all: creamy chowder-like soup, a flakey crust and minimal dish cleanup. It's for when you've got things to do and bags to chase, but want to put, you know, a meal on the table. Think of it as a pot pie without having to actually make . . . a pie.

2 tbsp (30 mL) olive oil

1 small onion, chopped

2 garlic cloves, minced

1 stalk celery, chopped

2 cups (500 mL) diced butternut squash

2 cups (500 mL) thinly sliced kale

½ cup (125 mL) chopped carrots

1 tsp (5 mL) dried thyme

½ tsp (2 mL) dried rosemary

Sea salt

⅓ cup (75 mL) unbleached all-purpose flour

1 can (14 oz/398 mL) cannellini (white kidney) beans, drained

3 cubes (each 1 tsp/5 mL) no-chicken or vegetable bouillon

1 bay leaf

3 cups (750 mL) water

1 cup + 2 tbsp (280 mL) unsweetened soy milk, divided

Freshly ground black pepper

2 sheets (10 inches/25 cm) vegan-friendly puff pastry dough, thawed if frozen

1 tsp (5 mL) pure maple syrup

1 Preheat the oven to 425°F (220°C).

2 In a large oven-safe skillet, heat olive oil over medium-high heat. Add onion and garlic; cook, stirring occasionally, for 3 to 5 minutes, until onion is translucent. Add celery, squash, kale, carrots, thyme, rosemary and a pinch of sea salt; cook for 5 minutes, or until kale is bright green.

3 Sprinkle in flour; stir to coat all veggies. Cook for 2 minutes, or until a paste forms. Add cannellini beans, bouillon and bay leaf. Slowly stir in water and 1 cup (250 mL) soy milk. Bring to a boil. Reduce heat to medium and simmer for 5 to 8 minutes, until veggies are tender and chowder is thickened slightly. Season to taste with sea salt and pepper. Remove from heat. Remove bay leaf.

4 Meanwhile, place puff pastry sheets on a work surface and roll out each into a 15-inch (38 cm) square. Cut out smaller 3-inch (7.5 cm) squares and place on top of the chowder, overlapping slightly.

5 In a small bowl, whisk together the remaining 2 tbsp (30 mL) soy milk and maple syrup. Brush the top of the pastry with the soy milk mixture.

6 Bake in the preheated oven for 5 to 10 minutes, until pastry begins to brown and the stew is bubbling.

7 Remove from the oven and let stand for 5 to 10 minutes before ladling chowder into bowls with lots of pastry crust.

$IDE HU$TLE

sīd \ 'hə-səl *(noun)*

1. A passion project or hobby you pursue alongside your day job, in hopes to escape the capitalist rat race. *"Martha thinks selling Monat is a side hustle. Who's going to tell her it's a pyramid scheme?"*

2. A small but delicious portion of food served alongside the main course. *"Look at those bomb potatoes and garlicky greens; this plate's got some serious side hustle."*

~~~~~~

They may sit on the edge of the plate, but these scrumptious companions are definitely not an afterthought. In my house, I make sure all sides are so well crafted, they could move into the starring role. These show-stopping dishes, from the crispy tofu to the fried rice, are all worthy of a round of applause and can even be paired with each other for an unforgettable meal.

BANGIN' SMASHED BROCCOLI

SERVES 4

We all have at least one vegetable we don't *love* but will tolerate because it's "good for you." This recipe is the result of me doing just that. I took broccoli (I'll deal, but it's just *so* treelike) and smothered it with something I love: a peanut buttery take on sweet and spicy bang bang sawse. My point? If you don't like something, just hide it under something you do love: veggies, tofu . . . And that goes for my feelings, too.

• RIMMED BAKING SHEET LINED WITH PARCHMENT PAPER

2 broccoli heads, cut into florets

3 tbsp (45 mL) olive oil

3 tbsp (45 mL) nutritional yeast

½ tsp (2 mL) sea salt

½ tsp (2 mL) freshly ground black pepper

BANG BANG SAUCE

¼ cup (60 mL) creamy peanut butter

3 tbsp (45 mL) sweet chili sauce

1 tbsp (15 mL) Sriracha sauce

⅓ cup (75 mL) boiling water

1 tsp (5 mL) sesame seeds

1 Preheat the oven to 425°F (220°C).

2 On the prepared baking sheet, toss broccoli with olive oil, nutritional yeast, sea salt and pepper. Spread out broccoli in a single layer and roast in the preheated oven for 10 minutes, tossing halfway, or until broccoli is tender and crisp.

3 **BANG BANG SAUCE** Meanwhile, in a small bowl, whisk together peanut butter, sweet chili sauce and Sriracha sauce. Add boiling water; whisk to combine. Set aside.

4 Remove the baking sheet from the oven. Using the back of a glass, press down on each broccoli floret firmly but carefully, making sure not to push so hard that the florets fall apart. Roast for another 10 minutes, or until broccoli is lightly charred and crispy.

5 Transfer broccoli to a serving dish, drizzle with two-thirds of the bang bang sauce and sprinkle with sesame seeds. Serve with the remaining bang bang sauce on the side for dipping.

HACK IT!

You know how some people don't just like Starbucks, they're obsessed with it? Well, I'm like that with bang bang sauce — it's unreal on almost anything. Try it as a dip for Practically Perfect Crispy Tofu (page 180), Southern-Style Popcorn Bites (page 121) or just any veggie you don't fully love. **Chef's kiss**

SHROOM RAIDER FRIED RICE

SERVES 4

The only thing more nostalgic to me than Super Mario 64 is the mushroom fried rice my mom would pick up at a local Chinese restaurant after a particularly rough week at work. I *love* mushrooms, so although the table was packed with tasty take-out faves, my go-to was always the dish packed with shrooms. These days, I just make it at home. It's a quick and easy use for your leftover cooked rice.

1 tbsp (15 mL) vegetable oil

8 oz (250 g) mushrooms of choice, chopped

1 small onion, chopped

3 garlic cloves, minced

3 tbsp (45 mL) toasted sesame oil, divided

1 large carrot, diced

1 cup (250 mL) frozen peas

3 cups (750 mL) cooked short-grain white rice

3 tbsp (45 mL) tamari or soy sauce (approx.)

1 to 2 tbsp (15 to 30 mL) I Put That Sh*t on Everything Chili Oil (page 196) or chili oil (optional)

2 green onions, white parts only, chopped

1   In a large skillet or wok, heat vegetable oil over medium-high heat. Add mushrooms, onion and garlic; cook, stirring constantly, for 5 to 7 minutes, until mushrooms are tender and browned slightly.

2   Add 1 tbsp (15 mL) sesame oil, carrot and peas; cook for 3 to 5 minutes, until carrot is tender and peas are thawed.

3   Add rice and stir to combine. Add tamari; stir until rice is well coated. Cook for 3 minutes, or until rice is warmed. Add the remaining 2 tbsp (30 mL) sesame oil and chili oil (if using); stir and cook for 3 minutes, or until rice has some crispy bits.

4   Stir in green onions and season with more tamari to taste, if necessary.

HACK IT!

Don't have tamari on hand? Just use soy sauce. Unless you're gluten-free — then you'll have to send your boo to the store.

10-MINUTE MOROCCAN-STYLE COUSCOUS

SERVES 4

It's the pasta so nice they named it twice. This easy, underrated side is savory and a little sweet, with distinctive Moroccan flavors. Nothing transports me back to Casablanca quite like the aroma of cumin, ginger, cinnamon and allspice — aka the spice blend ras el hanout — cooking together in perfect harmony. This recipe comes together in under 10 minutes, making it a fantastic weeknight side. Serve with my Easy Breezy Creamy Chic-Peas (page 143) or alongside my Lightning-Fast Mini Meatloaves (page 151).

2 tbsp (30 mL) olive oil

½ small onion, chopped

2 garlic cloves, minced

1 cup (250 mL) packed spinach, chopped

1 cube (1 tsp/5 mL) vegetable bouillon

1 tbsp (15 mL) ras el hanout

1 tbsp (15 mL) grated lemon zest

1¼ cups (310 mL) water

2 tbsp (30 mL) freshly squeezed lemon juice

1 cup (250 mL) couscous

Sea salt and freshly ground black pepper

2 tbsp (30 mL) chopped fresh parsley

1   In a medium saucepan, heat olive oil over medium-high heat. Add onion and garlic; cook, stirring occasionally, for 3 to 5 minutes, until onion is translucent.

2   Stir in spinach, bouillon, ras el hanout, lemon zest, water and lemon juice; bring to a boil. Add couscous, cover and remove from heat. Let stand for 5 minutes. Using a fork, fluff couscous. Season to taste with sea salt and pepper. Stir in parsley; serve.

PRACTICALLY PERFECT CRISPY TOFU

SERVES 4

This recipe is inspired by the crispy tofu cubes I consume by the bucket from a restaurant called Fresh in my hometown of Toronto. They are hella addictive, so I urge you to enter into this journey with caution. Once you pop, I promise you won't stop.

- **HIGH-POWERED BLENDER, FOOD PROCESSOR OR FOOD MILL**
- **LARGE HEAVY-BOTTOMED SAUCEPAN**
- **WIRE RACK OVER A RIMMED BAKING SHEET**

4 tsp (20 mL) garlic powder, divided

1 tsp (5 mL) onion powder

½ cup (125 mL) soy sauce

⅓ cup (75 mL) apple cider vinegar

3 tbsp (45 mL) water

1 tbsp (15 mL) pure maple syrup

1 tbsp (15 mL) chili sauce (optional)

2 packages (each 16 oz/450 g) firm or extra-firm tofu, pressed (page 15) and cubed

1 cup (250 mL) nutritional yeast

¾ cup (175 mL) panko bread crumbs

Vegetable oil

¼ cup (60 mL) cornstarch

Sesame seeds, for garnish (optional)

1. In a medium bowl, whisk together 1 tsp (5 mL) garlic powder, onion powder, soy sauce, apple cider vinegar, water, maple syrup and chili sauce (if using) to create a marinade. Add tofu cubes and toss to coat. Let stand for 15 minutes at room temperature or cover and place in the fridge for up to 2 hours.

2. Meanwhile, in the high-powered blender, combine nutritional yeast, bread crumbs and the remaining 1 tbsp (15 mL) garlic powder; pulse until even-sized crumbs form. Transfer to a medium bowl.

3. In a separate medium bowl, whisk together ¼ cup (60 mL) marinade, 1 tbsp (15 mL) vegetable oil and cornstarch. Add tofu and toss to coat. Transfer tofu to bread-crumb mixture and toss to coat.

4. Meanwhile, in the large heavy-bottomed saucepan, heat ½ inch (1 cm) vegetable oil over medium-high heat. Add tofu and cook for 1 to 2 minutes on each side, or until evenly browned. Transfer to the prepared wire rack — this will help keep them crispy!

5. Serve on top of cooked veggies, noodles or rice, in soups or my Massaman-Style Tofu Curry (page 154). You can also try them solo with your dip of choice, like my Freestyle Mayo (see page 118), Jalapeño Cheddar Dipping Sauce (see page 98) or Jerk Aioli (see page 148). Garnish with sesame seeds, if desired.

HACK IT!

TO BAKE Preheat the oven to 375°F (190°C) and line a rimmed baking sheet with parchment paper. Complete Step 3, transfer to the prepared baking sheet, then spray tofu lightly with cooking spray. Bake in the preheated oven for 20 to 25 minutes, flipping halfway, until evenly browned.

SIDEKICK SWEET FRIES

SERVES 4

A French fry is to a vegan what Robin is to Batman: the quintessential "What can I eat here?" sidekick when you've found yourself *(thanks to that friend who didn't bother to consider your dietary restrictions when picking a restaurant)* holding a menu that doesn't speak to your needs. From Burger King to haute cuisine, if there's nothing else veg-friendly on the menu, chances are there will be fries. Oh, and this recipe is made specifically with sweet potato — and baked — meaning these fries are pretty much a health food.

• 2 RIMMED BAKING SHEETS LINED WITH PARCHMENT PAPER

3 tbsp (45 mL) cornstarch

½ tsp (2 mL) onion powder

½ tsp (2 mL) garlic powder

½ tsp (2 mL) paprika

Sea salt

½ tsp (2 mL) freshly ground black pepper

2 large sweet potatoes, peeled and cut into ¼-inch (0.5 cm) thick sticks

3 tbsp (45 mL) olive oil

1   Preheat the oven to 400°F (200°C).

2   In a large bowl, combine cornstarch, onion powder, garlic powder, paprika, ½ tsp (2 mL) sea salt and pepper. Add sweet potatoes and toss to coat completely in the cornstarch mixture until almost no starch is left in the bowl. Add olive oil; toss to coat.

3   Arrange sweet potatoes on the prepared baking sheets in a single layer, spacing at least ½ inch (1 cm) apart.

4   Bake in the preheated oven for 15 minutes. Remove from the oven, flip and bake for another 5 to 10 minutes, until the fries are crispy and have begun to brown a bit at the tips.

5   Remove fries from the oven and let stand for 5 minutes on the baking sheet. (They will continue to crisp up as they cool.) Season to taste with sea salt and serve with your favorite dip, or try it with my Creamy Garlic Dipping Sauce (see page 98), Dill Sauce (see page 141) or ketchup.

MAKE IT SNAP! BLISTERED PEAS

SERVES 4

These peas were a total accident. For a while right after I adopted Kevin, my special needs dog, I wasn't sleeping well and would wake up at 3 a.m. hungry. I would put everything bagel seasoning on anything I could find in my kitchen: cucumbers, hummus, even bagels! One night I had a craving for edamame — but didn't have any — so I improvised with snap peas. The result was a crunchy, slightly sweet but salty bite with a hint of sesame. Proceed with caution . . . these are addictive!

1 tsp (5 mL) olive oil

1 lb (500 g) snap peas, trimmed

2 tsp (10 mL) toasted sesame oil

2 tbsp (30 mL) everything bagel seasoning

Freshly ground black pepper

1   In a large skillet, heat olive oil over high heat. Add snap peas and cook for 5 to 10 minutes, stirring occasionally, until blistered.

2   Remove from heat. Add sesame oil, everything bagel seasoning and a sprinkle of pepper; toss to coat. Serve. They also work as a side for Awesome Aussie Meat Pies (page 166) or as a fun appetizer served alongside Mixed Herb & Garlic Chèvre (page 111).

EVERY DAY I'M BRUSSELIN' CHIPS WITH TAHINI

SERVES 4

Kale chips have had their time in the spotlight and, quite frankly, they're a bit overrated. Make way for a new and exciting way to chip — Brussels sprouts! You know those handful of leaves that fall off when you're roasting Brussels in the oven? Well, they inspired these perfectly crispy bites of thinly sliced sprouts. Drizzled or dipped, these can be eaten on their own or as a side.

> **• RIMMED BAKING SHEET LINED WITH PARCHMENT PAPER**

2½ tsp (12 mL) garlic powder, divided

1½ tsp (7 mL) ground cumin

Sea salt

3 tbsp (45 mL) olive oil

2 tsp (10 mL) Dijon mustard

1½ lbs (750 g) Brussels sprouts, trimmed and thinly sliced

¼ cup (60 mL) tahini

¼ cup (60 mL) warm water (approx.)

1 tbsp (15 mL) freshly squeezed lemon juice

1   Preheat the oven to 400°F (200°C).

2   In a large bowl, whisk together 2 tsp (10 mL) garlic powder, cumin, ½ tsp (2 mL) sea salt, olive oil and Dijon. Add Brussels sprouts; toss to coat.

3   Spread Brussels sprouts on the prepared baking sheet in a single layer. Bake in the preheated oven for 15 to 20 minutes, flipping halfway, until crispy and browned.

4   Meanwhile, in a small bowl, whisk together tahini, warm water, lemon juice, the remaining ½ tsp (2 mL) garlic powder and a pinch of sea salt until smooth. Add more warm water 1 tsp (5 mL) at a time as needed to get a pourable sauce.

5   Remove Brussels sprouts from the oven. Season to taste with sea salt. Drizzle with some of the tahini sauce and serve with the remaining sauce on the side for dipping.

SWIPE RIGHT ROASTIES

SERVES 4

I may not be able to spice up your love life, but I sure as heck can get some spice on those potatoes. Unlike tonight's Hinge date, these bad boys are a sure thing. Each bite is like a concert of crispy tater with bursts of garlic and herbs. They go well with anything — as a base for gumbo (page 81) or with my Krabby Patty (page 138) — something else a dating app can't guarantee. I'm not saying you should replace men with potatoes . . . but aren't they already one and the same?

• 11- BY 7-INCH (28 BY 18 CM) GLASS BAKING DISH

1½ lbs (750 g) baby potatoes or fingerling potatoes, halved

Sea salt

⅓ cup (75 mL) olive oil

3 garlic cloves, minced

1 tsp (5 mL) dried rosemary

1 tsp (5 mL) dried parsley

1 tsp (5 mL) dried thyme

½ tsp (2 mL) freshly ground black pepper

Pinch red pepper flakes (optional)

1 Preheat the oven to 425°F (220°C).

2 Place potatoes in a large pot and add enough water to cover by 1 inch (2.5 cm). Add 1 tbsp (15 mL) sea salt and bring to a boil. Reduce heat to medium and simmer for 5 to 10 minutes, until just tender when pierced with a fork.

3 Meanwhile, pour olive oil into the baking dish. When potatoes have about 5 minutes left of cooking time, place baking dish in the oven for 5 minutes, or until oil is hot. Remove from the oven and whisk in garlic, rosemary, parsley, thyme, pepper and red pepper flakes (if using).

4 Drain potatoes and return to pot. Place over low heat for 1 to 2 minutes to remove excess moisture. Once pot is completely dry, cover and shake it. You want some of the potatoes to be just starting to fall apart.

5 Add potatoes to the casserole dish with the hot oil. Flip or move them around with a spatula to coat completely in oil. Sprinkle with ½ tsp (2 mL) sea salt.

6 Roast potatoes in the preheated oven for 20 to 25 minutes, turning once, until golden brown and crispy.

7 Remove from the oven and season to taste with salt and pepper; serve.

YOU NEED ME ZUCCHINI

SERVES 4 TO 6

You know that lonely zucchini that's always rolling around in your crisper like a forgotten middle child? I created a recipe to finally use it! This is the perfect blend of roasted veggies, with a touch of crisp from the nutritional yeast and a hint of melted cheese. Enjoy as a side with Bluenosin' Donairs (page 129) or Baby Back, Baby Back, Baby Back Rib Sammy (page 130). Then use leftovers in salads or pasta, or on pizza.

• RIMMED BAKING SHEET LINED WITH PARCHMENT PAPER

4 garlic cloves, minced

1 tbsp (15 mL) nutritional yeast

1¼ tsp (6 mL) Italian seasoning

¼ cup (60 mL) olive oil

1 medium green zucchini, cut into ½-inch (1 cm) slices

1 medium yellow zucchini, cut into ½-inch (1 cm) slices

1 red bell pepper, cut into ½-inch (1 cm) slices

1 lb (500 g) cherry tomatoes, halved

Sea salt and freshly ground black pepper

1 cup (250 mL) grated dairy-free Parmesan cheese (optional)

3 tbsp (45 mL) chopped flat-leaf (Italian) parsley

I Put That Sh*t on Everything Chili Oil (page 196) or chili oil (optional)

1   Preheat the oven to 400°F (200°C).

2   In a large bowl, whisk together garlic, nutritional yeast, Italian seasoning and olive oil. Add green zucchini, yellow zucchini, red pepper and tomatoes; gently toss to coat. Season to taste with sea salt and pepper.

3   Spread veggies on the prepared baking sheet in a single layer and sprinkle with dairy-free Parmesan cheese (if using). Bake in the preheated oven for 20 to 25 minutes, flipping halfway, until veggies are tender.

4   Season to taste with sea salt and pepper. Top with parsley and chili oil (if using) and serve alongside your favorite main.

HACK IT!

If you have any leftovers, throw them in with cooked pasta for a simple but incredible dish!

SIMPLY SUBLIME RICE WITH CILANTRO & LIME

SERVES 4 TO 6

As the great comedian Mitch Hedberg once said, "Rice is great if you're really hungry and want to eat two thousand of something." Now add garlic, cilantro and lime, and you've got the perfect base or side to almost any meal. Try it with Bean Cheesin' Tacos Dorados (page 114), Gratifying Okra Gumbo (page 81) or Mushroom Fajitas That Give a Sheet (page 150).

2 cups (500 mL) short-grain white rice

Water

1 garlic clove, smashed

1 bay leaf

Sea salt

½ cup (125 mL) chopped fresh cilantro

1 tsp (5 mL) grated lime zest

2 tbsp (30 mL) freshly squeezed lime juice

2 tsp (10 mL) freshly squeezed lemon juice

1 In a fine-mesh sieve, rinse rice with cold water until the water runs clear. Shake to remove any excess water.

2 Meanwhile, in a medium saucepan, bring 3 cups (750 mL) water to a boil. Stir in rice, garlic, bay leaf and 1 tsp (5 mL) sea salt. Reduce heat to low, cover and cook for 10 to 15 minutes, until all the water is absorbed. Remove from heat and let stand for 10 minutes. Do not remove the lid.

3 Using a fork, fluff the rice. Remove bay leaf, and gently stir in cilantro, lime zest, lime juice and lemon juice. Season to taste with sea salt.

EFFING GOOD SAUTÉED GREENS

SERVES 4 TO 6

I grew up in a house where we ate a lot of veggies. My mom is a bit of a health nut and was always no BS about food. Being picky at our dinner table and asking for Kraft Dinner just wasn't an option. Luckily for us kids, she made beyond-good greens. I've recreated the recipe here. I could easily scarf down a plate of these on their own as a meal, or alongside meat pies (page 166), meatloaf (page 151) or Swedish meatballs (page 165). You're welcome.

2 tbsp (30 mL) peanut or canola oil

4 garlic cloves, minced

Pinch red pepper flakes (optional)

3 cups (750 mL) trimmed and halved baby bok choy

3 cups (750 mL) lightly packed and coarsely chopped spinach leaves

3 cups (750 mL) lightly packed and coarsely chopped kale

1½ tbsp (22 mL) tamari

Sea salt and freshly ground black pepper

1. In a large skillet or wok, heat peanut oil over medium-high heat. Add garlic and red pepper flakes (if using); cook, stirring constantly, for 2 to 3 minutes, until garlic is golden.

2. Add baby bok choy, spinach and kale. Sprinkle with tamari; stir to coat. Cover with a lid and cook for 3 to 5 minutes, stirring frequently, until the greens are wilted and tender.

3. Season to taste with sea salt and pepper; serve.

I PUT THAT SH✳T ON EVERYTHING CHILI OIL

MAKES 2 CUPS (500 ML)

So, I'm standing there, vaxxed and waxed with a cart full of BBQ, jaw agape, offended by a vulgar price tag staring back at me: $12 for a jar of crispy chili oil?! Forget avocado toast — this is why millennials can't buy homes. Save yourself a down payment by cooking up this Chinese-inspired spicy, salty and savory oil at home. The umami will have you addicted and pouring it on everything from sandwiches to dessert.

1½ cups (375 mL) vegetable oil

4 small shallots, thinly sliced

6 garlic cloves, thinly sliced

1 tsp (5 mL) black peppercorns

1 cinnamon stick or 2 tsp (10 mL) ground cinnamon

One 2-inch (5 cm) piece gingerroot, peeled and minced

¼ cup (60 mL) red pepper flakes

2 tsp (10 mL) paprika

1 tsp (5 mL) brown sugar

1 tbsp (15 mL) tamari or soy sauce

1   In a small saucepan, bring vegetable oil, shallots, garlic, peppercorns and cinnamon stick to a gentle simmer over medium heat. Reduce heat to medium-low and simmer gently, stirring occasionally, for 25 to 30 minutes, until shallots and garlic are browned.

2   Meanwhile, in a medium heatproof glass bowl, combine ginger, red pepper flakes, paprika, brown sugar and tamari. Set aside.

3   Place a fine-mesh sieve over the heatproof glass bowl. Carefully strain the oil from the pan into the bowl, overtop the ginger mixture. Leave shallot mixture in the sieve and set aside to cool and crisp up, about 15 minutes.

4   Remove cinnamon stick from shallot mixture, then add mixture to the cooling oil. Let cool completely. You've got chili oil!

5   Transfer chili oil and crispy bits to a jar with a lid. Store in the fridge for up to 1 month.

Use this spinach as a filling for an omelet — it's super tasty!

DAS GERMAN CREAMED SPINACH

SERVES 4

Leave it to the Germans to take something as healthy as spinach and cream it! This stuff is the sh*t! It's known as *rahmspinat* in German, and it's cheap, frozen and available pretty much everywhere in Germany. It's the perfect easy side or, in Germany, after-school snack. In fact, when I moved to Canada, I spent years trying to figure out how to make my beloved spinach at home and — hurrah! — I've finally got it!

1 lb (500 g) frozen spinach, thawed

3 tbsp (45 mL) dairy-free butter

½ small onion, minced

3 tbsp (45 mL) unbleached all-purpose flour

1 cube (1 tsp/5 mL) vegetable bouillon

Pinch ground nutmeg

¾ **cup (175 mL)** unsweetened soy milk

1 bay leaf

Sea salt and freshly ground black pepper

1 In a fine-mesh sieve, place thawed spinach and press with the back of a wooden spoon (or anything you can push with) to squeeze out as much liquid as possible. Set aside.

2 In a medium saucepan, melt dairy-free butter over medium heat. Add onion; cook, stirring occasionally, for 3 to 5 minutes, until translucent.

3 Sprinkle in flour and whisk to combine. Cook, whisking constantly, for 4 to 5 minutes, until thickened and flour has turned light beige. (Congrats! You've made a roux!)

4 Stir in bouillon and nutmeg. Slowly pour in soy milk, whisking constantly, until bouillon has dissolved. Add bay leaf; bring to a boil, stirring constantly. Reduce heat to medium and simmer, stirring constantly, for 4 to 5 minutes, until thickened.

5 Remove bay leaf and add spinach to the saucepan. Cover and cook for another 3 to 5 minutes, until spinach is heated through. Season to taste with sea salt and pepper.

6 Serve alongside a protein-heavy main, potatoes and meatloaf (page 151), or tofu scramble.

HACK IT!

You can store this in an airtight container in the fridge for up to 5 days — not that it'll last that long. To reheat, simply warm spinach in a large skillet over medium-low heat for 5 to 8 minutes, until heated through.

POTENT POTA- BLES

ˈpō-t³nt \ ˈpō-tə-bəl *(noun)*

1. **Potent:** something that has a very strong effect. **Potables:** a liquid that you can safely drink, such as a smoothie, cocktail or hot drink. *The orange in this smoothie is so rich and fragrant! This potent potable's gotta be healthy!*

2. A popular category on *Jeopardy* referring to strong drinks. Kathie Lee Gifford: *"Um . . . Potent Potables? I'm sorry, I don't know what that [category] is."* Alex Trebek: *"It's . . . about alcohol."*

～～～～～～～～～～～～～～～～～～～～～～

Whether you're looking to sip a nutrient-packed smoothie, warm up with a hot cuppa white hot chocolate in month 11 of Canadian winter or get down on a Friday, the recipes on the next few pages will tickle your taste buds as well as quench your thirst.

Pair it with cardamom's subtle citrusy sweet aroma, and you've got a match made in cozy heaven.

CARDAMOM WHITE HOT CHOCOLATE FIT FOR A QUEEN

SERVES 2

Cardamom is known as the Queen of Spices. And Lord knows I love me a fabulous queen! Drag, feminist, royal, spice — all are invited to this extravaganza. Did you know that white chocolate isn't technically chocolate (it doesn't actually contain any chocolate solids)? This hot chocolate is super easy to make in your blender at home.

• HIGH-POWERED BLENDER

2½ cups (625 mL) unsweetened soy milk

2 tbsp (30 mL) coarsely chopped cacao butter

2 tbsp (30 mL) agave nectar or pure maple syrup (approx.)

1 tbsp (15 mL) tahini

¼ tsp (1 mL) ground cardamom

Pinch sea salt

½ tsp (2 mL) vanilla extract

OPTIONAL TOPPINGS

Vegan (gelatin-free) marshmallows or mini marshmallows

Dairy-free whipped topping

Ground cinnamon (optional)

1 In a small saucepan over medium heat, warm soy milk and cacao butter, until butter has melted, about 2 minutes.

2 Transfer soy milk mixture to the high-powered blender (reserving saucepan). Add agave nectar and tahini; blend on high speed until smooth.

3 Transfer soy milk mixture back to the reserved saucepan. Add cardamom and sea salt; slowly bring to a boil over medium-high heat, whisking constantly. Remove from heat.

4 Stir in vanilla. Taste and add more agave nectar for sweetness, if you like.

5 Pour hot chocolate into two mugs and top with vegan marshmallows, dairy-free whipped topping and/or a sprinkle of cinnamon (if using) and wake me up before you co-coa.

HACK IT!

Make this ho cho boozy by adding 1 oz (30 mL) whiskey or Baileys Almande, because it's always time for a cocktail!

HOMEMADE CHAI SYRUP

MAKES 2 CUPS (500 ML) CHAI SYRUP

Some things are just a crime against language and culture. Like saying "naan bread" (since "naan" means "bread") or "chai tea" (since "chai" means "tea"). And that's just as absurd as buying chai syrup for your iced lattes instead of making it at home by grinding your own spices for a tenth of the cost.

• MORTAR AND PESTLE

CHAI SYRUP

5 whole cloves

4 cardamom pods

1 star anise pod

¼ tsp (1 mL) fennel seeds

¼ tsp (1 mL) black peppercorns

¼ tsp (1 mL) ground nutmeg

2¼ cups (560 mL) water

⅔ cup (150 mL) agave nectar, organic granulated sugar or pure maple syrup

One 1-inch (2.5 cm) piece gingerroot, cut into pieces

4 black tea bags, cut open, or 4 tsp (20 mL) loose black tea leaves

1 cinnamon stick

1½ tsp (7 mL) vanilla extract

ICED LATTE (OPTIONAL)

Ice cubes

1 cup (250 mL) unsweetened non-dairy milk

1 In the mortar and pestle, coarsely crush cloves, cardamom, star anise, fennel and peppercorns. Add nutmeg; set aside.

2 In a small saucepan, bring water and agave nectar to a boil over medium-high heat. Reduce heat to medium-low and add ginger, black tea leaves, clove mixture and cinnamon stick. Cover and simmer for 20 minutes.

3 Remove the saucepan from the heat and strain the tea-infused syrup through a fine-mesh sieve into a medium heatproof bowl. Stir in vanilla. Let syrup cool completely, then pour into a sealable jar. Make an iced latte (see Step 4) or store syrup in the fridge for up to 1 month (see *Hack It!*).

4 **TO MAKE YOUR ICED LATTE (OPTIONAL)** Fill a tall glass or mason jar halfway with ice cubes. Add 2 tbsp to ¼ cup (30 to 60 mL) chai syrup, depending on how sweet you want your iced latte, and top with non-dairy milk. Enjoy!

HACK IT!

Cutting open tea bags and sprinkling the tea leaves directly in the water, rather than using the tea bags, makes for a more aromatic tea. Trust.

Want to make your syrup last longer? Add 1 oz (30 mL) vodka to the cooled syrup to extend its life in the fridge for up to 3 months.

Use this syrup in place of simple syrup in cocktails for a soul-warming libation.

EASY AF SANGRIA

SERVES 1

To all you wine snobs out there, this recipe might sound freaking insane, but you know what else is insane? Making a 12-ingredient sangria that takes 45 minutes to prepare and lasts for 5, tops. All you need to do here is add some orange or lemon soda to a glass of red wine and presto! You've got yourself a sangria for one!

4 ice cubes

¾ cup (175 mL) red wine, chilled

½ cup (125 mL) sweet orange or lemon soda

1 orange slice (optional)

1   Put ice cubes in a wine glass. Pour in wine, top with orange soda and garnish with an orange slice (if using). Enjoy on a budget.

TROPICAL CONTACT HIGH

SERVES 1

When living through a global pandemic, one must always be armed with the essentials: a mask, hand sanitizer and a Rolodex of cocktail recipes to help you escape the four walls you've been staring at during isolation. This tropical libation has been a go-to. It's a cocktail inspired by the classic Shirley Temple, with a sweet but tart grapefruit twist — perfect for watching the world open up while you're stuck at home feeling vacation adjacent.

• HIGHBALL GLASS

4 ice cubes

1½ oz (45 mL) tequila

2 tbsp (30 mL) freshly squeezed lime juice

1½ tsp (7 mL) grenadine

¾ cup (175 mL) sweetened grapefruit soda

1 grapefruit segment (optional)

1 maraschino cherry (optional)

1   Put ice cubes in the highball glass. Pour in tequila, lime juice and grenadine; top with grapefruit soda, and stir gently.

2   Garnish with a grapefruit segment and a maraschino cherry (if using) and do some beach daydreaming.

CREAMSICLE DREAM SMOOTHIE

SERVES 1

This creamsicle is a dreamsicle. It's fruity and creamy, with that Orange Julius sweetness you know and love. Pair it with my Food Court Orange Cauliflower (page 140) and do some online shopping for a perfect day at the mall — from home.

• HIGH-POWERED BLENDER

¾ **cup (175 mL)** unsweetened non-dairy milk

1 tsp (5 mL) grated orange zest

1 orange, peeled and broken into segments

½ **cup (125 mL)** frozen mango chunks

1 scoop vanilla protein powder (optional)

⅛ **tsp (0.5 mL)** ground turmeric

Pinch sea salt

1 tsp (5 mL) vanilla extract

1   In the high-powered blender, combine non-dairy milk, orange zest, orange, mango, vanilla protein powder (if using), turmeric, sea salt and vanilla; blend on high speed until smooth. Pour into a glass; serve.

SON OF A PEACH

SERVES 1

This peachy take on a Moscow mule tastes just like a Southern belle raisin' some hell. However, don't let the sweet taste fool you: this drink packs a serious punch. One or two will make you feel warm and fuzzy, but drink responsibly because after five or six, tomorrow's gonna be the pits.

- **MINI FOOD PROCESSOR (OPTIONAL)**
- **HIGHBALL GLASS OR COPPER MUG**
- **COCKTAIL SHAKER**

½ large peach, pitted

Ice cubes

1½ oz (45 mL) bourbon

1 tbsp (15 mL) freshly squeezed lime juice

¾ cup (175 mL) ginger beer

3 peach slices (optional)

1 lime slice (optional)

1 In the mini food processor (or using a fork and small bowl), purée peach. Set aside.

2 Add 3 ice cubes to the highball glass.

3 Add a handful of ice cubes to the cocktail shaker. Add peach purée and any juices leftover in the food processor (or bowl) — it's the good stuff. Add bourbon and lime juice. Shake well and strain the mixture into the glass.

4 Top with ginger beer and garnish with slices of peach and lime (if using).

SUGAR HIGH

ˈshu̇-gər \ h *(noun)*

1. **Sugar high:** A sudden feeling of happiness, lightness and euphoria after eating a really incredible treat or dessert. Signs of a sugar high include excitement, talking quickly, running, jumping and a passionate need to post on TikTok. *Jenn: "What's up with her?" Louis: "She's got that watermelon sugar high!"*

~~~~~~~~~~~~~~~~~~~~~~~~~~~~~~~~~~~~

I'm sorry, breakfast, lunch and dinner, but dessert is undoubtedly the best meal of the day. Don't get me wrong, the necessary three main meals are great, and they will satisfy you, but they're more utilitarian, while dessert is just 100% pure fun. It has one, and only one, purpose — to bring you joy! So go ahead, find happiness among the Tim's Chocolate-Glazed Bites (page 219), a piece of Berry French Custard Tart (page 232) or a few chewy cookies (pages 223 and 227) because, baby girl, it's time to treat yo'self!

BELGIUM COOKIE BUTTER

MAKES 1 CUP (250 ML)

I've got 99 problems, and 86 of them are completely made-up scenarios I'm stressing about for no logical reason. Oh, you too? The answer, my friend, is Biscoff cookie butter. Whether anxiety's got you reeling or depression's got you feeling the type of blues that make even biting into a cookie seem like a chore right now, this dreamy, silky smooth, caramel, gingerbread butter is like Zoloft in a jar.

• FOOD PROCESSOR

1½ cups (375 mL) vegan-friendly Biscoff cookie crumbs

2 tbsp (30 mL) brown sugar

½ cup (125 mL) unsweetened non-dairy milk

1 tsp (5 mL) vanilla extract

½ tsp (2 mL) ground cinnamon

Sea salt

⅓ cup (75 mL) refined coconut oil, at room temperature

1   In a small saucepan, combine Biscoff cookie crumbs, brown sugar, non-dairy milk, vanilla, cinnamon and a pinch of sea salt. Cook over medium heat, whisking constantly, until the crumbs and sugar have dissolved. The mixture should be smooth and thickened slightly and resemble a batter.

2   Transfer cookie "batter" to the food processor. Let stand for 3 to 5 minutes to cool slightly. Add coconut oil and process until smooth.

3   Transfer to a container with a lid and let stand, uncovered, to cool completely.

4   Cover and store in the fridge for up to 10 days. Enjoy on toast, serve with fruit, add to milkshakes, blizzards or banana bread — or just enjoy by the spoonful.

HACK IT!

Try Oreos in this cookie butter! Use the same amount of crumbled Oreos and leave out the Biscoff crumbs, brown sugar and cinnamon. (The Oreo filling will add more than enough sweetness.) Proceed with the recipe as directed.

TIM'S CHOCOLATE-GLAZED BITES

MAKES 24 DONUT HOLES

For those of you who may not know, a Timbit is a branded version of a donut hole from one of Canada's most beloved coffee franchises, Tim Hortons. There's an unwritten rule here that if you arrive late but bring a box of assorted Timbits, you can't get in trouble. I've saved you the inevitable drama of the least-favorite flavors being left to go stale at the bottom of the box by giving you only my best version, the classic — the chocolate-glazed glory.

- **ELECTRIC MIXER**
- **24-CUP MINI MUFFIN TIN OR DONUT HOLE PAN, GREASED**
- **WIRE RACK OVER A RIMMED BAKING SHEET**

1¼ cups (310 mL) unbleached all-purpose flour, sifted

½ cup (125 mL) packed brown sugar

⅓ cup (75 mL) unsweetened cocoa powder, sifted

¾ tsp (3 mL) baking powder

½ tsp (2 mL) baking soda

¼ tsp (1 mL) sea salt

½ cup (125 mL) dairy-free butter or margarine

½ cup (125 mL) plain dairy-free yogurt

2 tsp (10 mL) vanilla extract

½ cup (125 mL) unsweetened soy milk, divided

1½ cups (375 mL) confectioners' (icing) sugar, sifted

1 Preheat the oven to 350°F (180°C).

2 In a large bowl, whisk together flour, brown sugar, cocoa, baking powder, baking soda and sea salt.

3 In the bowl of the stand mixer fitted with the paddle attachment (or in a large bowl using an electric hand mixer), cream together dairy-free butter, dairy-free yogurt and vanilla. Beat in ¼ cup (60 mL) soy milk, followed by the flour mixture, until smooth.

4 Spoon batter into the prepared mini muffin tin, filling each cup about three-quarters full. Bake in the preheated oven for 15 minutes, or until a tester inserted into the center of a donut hole comes out clean. Let cool in the tin for about 5 minutes to set, then transfer each donut hole to the prepared wire rack.

5 Meanwhile, in a medium bowl, whisk together confectioners' sugar and the remaining ¼ cup (60 mL) soy milk, until runny. That's how you make glaze!

6 While the donut holes are still warm but cool enough to touch, dip them one at a time into the glaze and then place back on the wire rack so any excess glaze can drip off onto the baking sheet. Let glaze cool completely. Serve with afternoon coffee or tea, or pop one in your mouth when you need your 3 p.m. sugar fix. You can store these donut holes at room temperature in an airtight container for up to 3 days.

"I'M BUSY" OREO BLIZZARDS

SERVES 2

There is no feeling of relief like the one you get after sending an "I'm sorry, I can't make it tonight" text. I take "Netflix and chill" literally. It's a luxury. I take off my bra, perfectly mix smashed Oreos into creamy soft ice cream and plop my butt onto the sofa. Listen, it's not that I don't want to get blasted off $4 margaritas and cry in a public bathroom with my frands, it's just that some nights I'd rather stay at home, watch a murder documentary and face-fist a DQ Blizzard–inspired treat.

• STAND MIXER OR FOOD PROCESSOR (OPTIONAL; SEE *HACK IT!*)

2 cups (500 mL) dairy-free vanilla ice cream

1¼ cups (310 mL) coarsely chopped Oreos (approx.), divided

1   Place the bowl of the stand mixer (or of a food processor) in the freezer for 10 minutes to chill.

2   Add dairy-free ice cream to the chilled bowl. Using the paddle attachment of the stand mixer on medium speed (or pulsing in the food processor), beat until softened. Add 1 cup (250 mL) Oreos; beat (or pulse) to combine.

3   Transfer to tall glasses to get that DQ look, or to dessert bowls, and garnish each with about 2 tbsp (30 mL) chopped Oreos. Feel free to add more if want some extra — I always do!

HACK IT!

Don't have a stand mixer or food processor? No problem! Just use a large, chilled freezer-safe bowl, a wooden spoon and some elbow grease.

Try this with any chocolate candy or treat you love. Dairy-free peanut butter cups and cheesecake are two of my other favorites.

These are my favorite cookies of all time.

SOFT & ZINGY GINGER MOLASSES COOKIES

MAKES 15 COOKIES

If I had a dollar for every ginger molasses cookie I ate during lockdown, I'd have enough money to buy a house . . . in this economy. Most people are more about that hip chocolate chip, but I promise you, these are not your nana's gingersnaps. These are more like the bold gingerbread-spiced, chewy and perfectly undercooked cookies baked at your favorite hipster café.

- **ELECTRIC MIXER**
- **2 RIMMED BAKING SHEETS LINED WITH PARCHMENT PAPER**

2¼ cups (560 mL) unbleached all-purpose flour

1 tbsp (15 mL) ground ginger

1½ tsp (7 mL) ground cinnamon

1½ tsp (7 mL) baking soda

½ tsp (2 mL) ground cloves

¼ tsp (1 mL) ground nutmeg

¾ cup (175 mL) salted dairy-free butter or margarine, at room temperature (see *Hack It!*)

½ cup (125 mL) packed brown sugar

¼ cup (60 mL) organic granulated sugar

¼ cup (60 mL) light (fancy) molasses

3 tbsp (45 mL) aquafaba (page 15)

2 tsp (10 mL) vanilla extract

1 cup (250 mL) coarse sugar, such as turbinado

1. In a large bowl, whisk together flour, ginger, cinnamon, baking soda, cloves and nutmeg. Set aside.

2. In the bowl of the stand mixer fitted with the paddle attachment (or in a large bowl using an electric hand mixer), cream together dairy-free butter, brown sugar and granulated sugar. Add molasses and beat until fluffy. Add aquafaba and vanilla; beat to combine, scraping down the sides of the bowl as necessary. Gradually beat in flour mixture until combined.

3. Cover the bowl with plastic wrap or foil and chill in the fridge for at least 30 minutes or up to 5 days. If the cookie dough is chilled longer than 2 hours, let stand at room temperature for about 30 minutes before baking or else the cookies will not spread properly.

4. Preheat the oven to 350°F (180°C).

5. Put coarse sugar in a small bowl.

6. Scoop out 2 tbsp (30 mL) dough and roll into a ball. Repeat until all the dough is used up. Roll the balls in the bowl of coarse sugar to coat completely. Place on the prepared baking sheets about 3 inches (7.5 cm) apart. Using your hands, press to flatten the cookies slightly.

7. Bake in the preheated oven for 7 minutes, or until edges are set and cracks begin to form on the top. Remove the baking sheets from the oven and gently bang on the counter a couple of times. Return to the oven and bake for another 3 minutes.

8. Remove the baking sheets from the oven and bang on the counter again to flatten cookies. Let the cookies cool on the baking sheet for about 5 minutes, then transfer to a wire rack. Store cookies in an airtight container at room temperature for up to 4 days.

HACK IT!

If you are using unsalted dairy-free butter or margarine, add ½ tsp (2 mL) sea salt in Step 1.

S'MORES CUPCAKES

MAKES 20 CUPCAKES

A s'more and a cupcake in one final form! Diet starts never! As a woman who grew up in the heroin-chic era, I can't say I am sad to see the slow death of diet culture. Call me crazy, but I'd rather eat whatever I want. We are all better and bolder than restrictive eating, and I encourage you to eat s'*more* of what you crave. May I suggest these chocolate-filled, marshmallow fluff–topped cupcakes, a glass of bubbly and playing with fire?

- **TWO 12-CUP MUFFIN TINS LINED WITH PAPER LINERS**
- **ELECTRIC MIXER**
- **LARGE PIPING BAG FITTED WITH THE 1M OPEN STAR TIP (OPTIONAL)**
- **KITCHEN TORCH (OPTIONAL)**

1 package (about 18 oz/560 g) chocolate cake mix

¾ cup (175 mL) vegan-friendly graham cracker crumbs, divided

1½ cups (375 mL) club soda

⅓ cup (75 mL) vegetable oil

⅓ cup (75 mL) aquafaba (page 15)

1 tsp (5 mL) vanilla extract

¼ tsp (1 mL) cream of tartar

2 tbsp (30 mL) water

1 package (10 oz/300 g) vegan (gelatin-free) mini marshmallows

¼ cup (60 mL) confectioners' (icing) sugar, sifted

1½ cups (375 mL) dairy-free semisweet chocolate chips or chopped chocolate

2 tbsp (30 mL) refined coconut oil

1   In a large bowl, combine cake mix, ½ cup (125 mL) graham cracker crumbs, club soda and vegetable oil. Using a spoon, evenly divide batter among muffin cups, filling them about three-quarters full.

2   Bake in the preheated oven for 18 to 20 minutes, until a tester inserted into the center of a cupcake comes out clean. Place muffin tin on a wire rack until cool enough to handle. Transfer each cupcake to the wire rack.

3   Preheat the oven to 350°F (180°C).

4   In the bowl of the stand mixer fitted with the wire whip attachment (or in a large bowl using an electric hand mixer), whip aquafaba, vanilla and cream of tartar for about 10 minutes on high speed, until fluffy peaks form. It should look like a meringue.

5   Meanwhile, in a medium microwave-safe bowl, combine water and vegan marshmallows. Microwave in 30-second intervals, stirring in between, until melted.

6   Add melted marshmallows and confectioners' sugar to the aquafaba mixture and whip on high speed until smooth. Cover.

7   Place dairy-free chocolate in a small microwave-safe bowl. Microwave on High in 30-second intervals, stirring in between, until melted. Stir in coconut oil until melted and combined. Look at you go! You've just made ganache!

8   Using your finger, gently press down the center of each cupcake halfway, forming a pocket, and spoon ganache into each.

9   Transfer marshmallow meringue to the piping bag (or place in a large sealable bag with a corner cut off). Pipe in a circle on each cupcake.

10 Using the torch at full blast, holding it about 3 inches (7.5 cm) from the surface of the meringue, lightly brown the top. (If you don't own a kitchen torch, preheat the broiler. Place cupcakes on a rimmed baking sheet. Position on the top rack of the oven and broil for 30 seconds to 1 minute, until lightly browned on top. This can go from perfect to burnt in a matter of seconds, so watch it carefully.)

11 Evenly sprinkle the remaining ¼ cup (60 mL) graham cracker crumbs (if desired) over cupcakes.

HACK IT!

Can't find vegan-friendly graham crackers? No problem. Use Biscoff cookies! They're almost always vegan. Just make sure to check the ingredients.

Lessen your load by baking the cupcakes the day before serving, and then preparing the rest of the recipe the day of.

I DID IT ALL FOR THE CHOCOLATE CHIP OATMEAL COOKIE . . .

MAKES 1 DOZEN COOKIES

Admittedly, I'm not the biggest fan of oatmeal. But what I lack in oatmeal interest, I make up for with my passion for cookies. I mean, aren't most things better in the form of a sweet, buttery, chewy cookie? Well, this classic oatmeal chocolate chip cookie recipe is all that and a sprinkle of sea salt. Think of it as a gourmet level up, leaving your taste buds with a delightful surprise.

- **ELECTRIC MIXER**
- **RIMMED BAKING SHEET LINED WITH PARCHMENT PAPER**

1½ cups (375 mL) large-flake (old-fashioned) rolled oats

1 tsp (5 mL) baking powder

½ tsp (2 mL) cornstarch

½ tsp (2 mL) ground cinnamon

½ cup (125 mL) dairy-free butter or margarine, softened

⅔ cup (150 mL) organic granulated sugar

⅓ cup (75 mL) packed brown sugar

3 tbsp (45 mL) aquafaba (page 15)

2 tsp (10 mL) vanilla extract

¾ cup (175 mL) unbleached all-purpose flour

½ cup (125 mL) dairy-free semisweet chocolate chips

Flakey sea salt or sea salt

1. In a large bowl, whisk together oats, baking powder, cornstarch and cinnamon. Set aside.

2. In the bowl of the stand mixer fitted with the paddle attachment (or in a large bowl using an electric hand mixer), cream together dairy-free butter, granulated sugar and brown sugar on high speed. Add aquafaba and vanilla; beat to combine, scraping down the sides of the bowl as necessary. Add oat mixture and beat to combine. Add flour and beat until just combined. Fold in the dairy-free chocolate chips and place in the fridge for 15 minutes.

3. Preheat the oven to 350°F (180°C).

4. Scoop out 2 tbsp (30 mL) dough and roll into a ball. Repeat until all the dough is used up. Place on the prepared baking sheet about 2½ inches (6 cm) apart. Using your hands, press to flatten the cookies slightly.

5. Bake in the preheated oven for 7 minutes, or until cookie edges appear set but the center feels undercooked. Remove the baking sheet from the oven and gently bang on the counter a couple of times. Sprinkle the tops with a pinch of flakey sea salt and return to the oven for another 2 to 3 minutes, until golden at the edges but still undercooked in the center. Always err on the side of undercooked for a soft chewy cookie.

6. Remove from the oven and let the cookies cool on the baking sheet for about 5 minutes. Transfer to a wire rack to cool completely.

HACK IT!

Change things up by replacing the dairy-free chocolate chips with the same amount of raisins, cranberries, nuts or . . . wait for it . . . vegan (gelatin-free) mini marshmallows.

THE 45-MINUTE BIRTHDAY CAKE

SERVES 12

Have you ever forgotten someone's birthday and the rushed gift you bought at the gas station didn't wow them? Well, you're not alone. So here I am to save you (and me) from ever running into this problem again. Keep prepared cake mix, frosting and canned soda in the back of your pantry in case of emergency, and in under an hour, you can make someone a sweet and colorful birthday treat.

- **ELECTRIC MIXER**
- **TWO 9-INCH (23 CM) SPRINGFORM PANS LINED WITH PARCHMENT PAPER AND GREASED**

2 packages (each about 18 oz/560 g) confetti cake mix

2 cans (each 12 oz/355 mL) orange soda

2 containers (each 12 oz/340 g) prepared vegan-friendly whipped vanilla frosting (see *Hack It!*)

2 tbsp (30 mL) grated orange zest

OPTIONAL TOPPINGS

Sprinkles

Coconut flakes

1 Preheat the oven to 350°F (180°C).

2 In the bowl of the stand mixer fitted with the wire whip attachment (or in a large bowl using a whisk), whip together cake mix and orange soda on medium speed until just combined.

3 Evenly divide batter between the prepared springform pans. Using a spatula, smooth out the tops.

4 Bake in the preheated oven for 25 to 30 minutes, until a tester inserted into the center comes out clean.

5 Meanwhile, in the clean bowl of the stand mixer fitted with the wire whip attachment (or in a large bowl using an electric hand mixer), beat vanilla frosting and orange zest on high speed until fluffy. Chill in the fridge while you prepare the rest of the recipe. Remove about 10 minutes before icing the cake, to let it warm up a bit.

6 Remove cakes from the oven and let cool completely in the pans.

7 Carefully remove the first cake from the pan and place it on a cake stand or plate. (If the top has an obvious curve, trim it flat with a very sharp knife.) Generously frost the top of the cake. Carefully remove the second cake from the pan and place it on top of the first. Frost the top of the cake and the sides of both. Decorate with toppings (if using). Serve or store in the fridge for up to 3 days.

HACK IT!

Add 1 tsp (5 mL) grated orange zest or flavored extract to give your icing extra depth and flavor.

Use different flavored sodas to make fun combinations — like club soda and yellow cake mix to make a basic cake, root beer and chocolate cake mix to make a root beer float cake and grape soda and vanilla cake mix to make a purple grape–flavored cake.

You'll even have time to write a really nice card.

CHIPSY MARSHMALLOW TREATS

MAKES 1 DOZEN SQUARES

As a person who often craves snacks but doesn't keep many in the house, I can appreciate the weirdness of this recipe. The juxtaposition of flavors you get from mixing rippled chips and marshmallows was clearly created by someone who was either burning one down or heavily PMS-ing. They're sweet yet salty, kind of like my personality when Aunt Flo pays a visit. They'll take you about 15 minutes to make and even less to finish the entire pan.

> **• 9-INCH (23 CM) SQUARE METAL BAKING PAN, GREASED**

¼ cup (60 mL) dairy-free butter or margarine

1 package (10 oz/300 g) vegan (gelatin-free) marshmallows

1 tsp (5 mL) vanilla extract

1 package (8 oz/200 g) rippled plain potato chips, lightly crushed into large pieces

1 In a large saucepan over medium heat, melt dairy-free butter. Add marshmallows and stir to combine.

2 Remove from heat and stir in vanilla. Add potato chips and stir until well coated.

3 Add the mixture to the prepared pan. Using a spatula or greased fingers, press down evenly. Place in the fridge for about 15 minutes, until hardened.

4 Cut into squares and serve. Store leftovers at room temperature in an airtight container for up to 7 days.

HACK IT!

For a tasty twist, use peanut butter instead of dairy-free butter or margarine, and/or drizzle 2 to 3 tbsp (30 to 45 mL) melted dairy-free bittersweet chocolate overtop before chilling.

BERRY FRENCH CUSTARD TART

SERVES 8 TO 10

Arrête de ramener sa fraise is French for "No one asked you" or "Mind your business." Translated literally it means "stop bringing back your strawberry," but it is also a casual way of saying "Come on! Join us!" How typically French to have the same saying for both a rebuff and an invitation. This simple yet impressive tart is filled with buttery pastry cream and fresh strawberries and topped with glaze.

One 9-inch (23 cm) vegan-friendly pie shell, thawed

3 cups (750 mL) unsweetened soy milk, divided

½ cup (125 mL) cornstarch

½ cup (125 mL) organic granulated sugar

¼ cup (60 mL) dairy-free butter or margarine, softened

2 tsp (10 mL) grated lemon zest

1½ tsp (7 mL) vanilla extract

1½ cups (375 mL) fresh strawberries, sliced

3 tbsp (45 mL) smooth strawberry jelly or jam (see *Hack It!*)

1½ tbsp (22 mL) freshly squeezed lemon juice

1. Preheat the oven to 375°F (190°C).

2. Poke pie shell all over with a fork and cover with foil. Bake in the preheated oven for 10 minutes. Remove foil and bake for about 3 minutes, until shell is golden. Set aside.

3. Meanwhile, in a small bowl, whisk together 1 cup (250 mL) soy milk and cornstarch. Set aside.

4. In a medium saucepan, bring the remaining 2 cups (500 mL) soy milk and sugar to a gentle boil over medium-high heat. Slowly whisk in cornstarch mixture until smooth. Immediately reduce heat to medium and simmer for 3 to 4 minutes, whisking constantly, until mixture has thickened. Remove from heat.

5. Whisk in dairy-free butter, lemon zest and vanilla. Voilà! It's pastry cream! Transfer to a medium bowl to cool slightly.

6. Pour pastry cream into pie shell and use the back of a spoon to smooth. Arrange strawberries on top of the pastry cream in a circular pattern, lining the outer edge and then moving inward with a slight overlap, sort of like scalloped potatoes.

7. Meanwhile, in a small saucepan, heat strawberry jam and lemon juice over medium-high heat. Cook, whisking constantly, until simmering. Remove from heat and brush over the strawberries.

8. Loosely cover tart and place in the fridge for a minimum of 2 hours or up to 3 days, until the pastry cream has settled and stiffened slightly. Serve.

HACK IT!

Can't find jam without fruit pieces? No problem! Push the glaze through a fine-mesh sieve to remove the chunks.

ACKNOWLEDGMENTS

A VERY SPECIAL THANKS TO EVERYONE WHO MADE THIS BOOK HAPPEN.

Despite writing these pages during a global pandemic, I never once felt isolated. So many brains, hands and taste buds worked together to create this special addition to your kitchen.

I am sure I have missed, or failed to mention, some who have inspired and supported me over the years. I would like to start with a collective thanks to all of you under that category.

Then I'd like to thank (blame) all my Edgy Veg viewers, readers and fans for not-so-politely demanding a second book. Without your support, I would not be here sharing my passion for cooking and compassion for animals — you are the gas that keeps this plant-based engine running.

Many people helped to bring these recipes together, but my incredible assistant-turned-friend Molly Fleming was by my side every step of the way. I could not have done this without you. Thank you for your dedication and hard work, testing every single recipe that went into this book, especially during the period when I lost my taste and smell after succumbing to Covid-19. Your patience is unmatched, and I am forever grateful for your unique brand of funny and for picking up the creative slack when I could no longer construct coherent puns or dad jokes.

To the entire DMG team: A huge shout-out to you all for keeping me organized and on task, especially during the weeks my ADD took over and I found myself overwhelmed. Your continued hard work has helped me realize my dreams and kept my business running smoothly as I dedicated a year of my life to writing this book. To Anthony, my manager, my friend, my partner in crime, my ride or die: Thanks for always having my back and for your fierce dedication to my vision. I am forever indebted to you.

To my incredible photography team: Brilynn Ferguson, your stunning photos brought my recipes to life once again. Your ability to make me feel calm and confident is a true art form, and there is nobody else I would rather spend time with in the studio. To my fantastic stylists, Chef Char and Adam Ward: Working in the studio with you was an absolute pleasure. You easily and flawlessly turned my visions into a reality, all while making my stomach hurt with laughs and lots of dancing. Techno marching bands forever! I'd like to extend my gratitude to Laura Branson and the team at Propaganda.

You truly have created magical heaven for Toronto food stylists. Thank you for your continued support of my second book.

To the entire Robert Rose team: Thank you for embarking on this journey with me again. To my fantastic editors, Meredith and Michelle: Thank you for the many hours, back and forths, and for putting up with my stubbornness. You 100% made my deep hatred for numerous rounds of editing tolerable. I am so proud of what we have created together.

To my friends and family: Thank you for allowing me to share my passions with you all. Your ongoing support means more than I could ever express on this page — cheers to the many meals we have had and will continue to indulge in together. I will always find joy in the shared experience of eating with you. Every one of you is a muse.

To my partner, Louis: A huge thank you for helping me convert all recipes from metric to imperial. It is a thankless and tedious task, and you killed it so I wouldn't have to do it myself. Much like in our daily life, you took a dreaded job off my plate so I could focus on what I love. Thank you for trying every dish experiment, no matter how questionable or strange, and for allowing me to share my passion for compassion with you. Above all, I would like to thank you for your patience and love. You have been my biggest cheerleader through this entire process. Thank you for picking up the slack at home when I dove deep into writing madness.

And last but not certainly least, thank you to my four canine children, Harley, Winston, Kevin and Mr. Frederickson, for their daily lessons and numerous cuddles. Dogs (and all animals) always seem to let go of the past and live every day with joy, compassion and play. This is something we, as humans, should all strive for. All animals, no matter their species, deserve love and respect, and I will not end this journey until each and every one of them is free.

INDEX

H

herbs. *See also* cilantro
  Ah, Freak Out! Le Freak, C'est Greek!, 56
  Avocado Caprese, 22
  Impasta Pesto Salad, 53
  Linguine Aglio e Olio, 169
  Mixed Herb & Garlic Chèvre, 111
  Ostentatious Olives, 105
Higher Morels Creamy Mushroom Soup, 80
Homemade Chai Syrup, 204
Hot Pot Pie Simmer, 173
hot sauces (as ingredient)
  Bang Bang Sauce, 177
  Essence of the Sea Po'boy, 162
  Freestyle Fries, 118
  I'm Drunk! Noodles!, 157
Houston! We've Got Huevos!, 30
hummus
  Fancy Fall Charcuterie Board, 109
  It's Just a Grilled Caesar! Romaine Calm!, 58
  Onions 'n' Hummus, 23

I

I Did It All for the Chocolate Chip Oatmeal Cookie, 227
I'd Like S'amore Garlic Bread & Pizza Dippers, 98
"I'm Busy" Oreo Blizzards, 220
I'm Drunk! Noodles!, 157
Impasta Pesto Salad, 53
I Put That Sh*t on Everything Chili Oil, 196
It'll Make You Quake, Oatmeal Cake, 34
It's Just a Grilled Caesar! Romaine Calm!, 58

J

Jalapeño Cheddar Dipping Sauce, 98
Jerk-Seasoned Chickpea Tacos with Pineapple Slaw, 148

K

kala namak, 15

kale. *See also* greens
  The Divorced Dad's Dill-Icious Vegan Dinner, 141
  Hot Pot Pie Simmer, 173
  No-Fail Kale Miso Slaw, 65
Kimchi Cute-Cumber Salad, 50
Krabby Patty, 138

L

Labor-Saving Lentil Soup, 90
Lazy Lasagna, 126
lemon
  Berry French Custard Tart, 232
  It'll Make You Quake, Oatmeal Cake, 34
  Ostentatious Olives, 105
  10-Minute Moroccan-Style Couscous, 179
lentils
  Eggs & the City Omelet, 38
  The Gooey Messy Lentil Burger aka Sloppy Joe, 147
  Labor-Saving Lentil Soup, 90
lettuce
  Crunchy Chalupa Tacos, 153
  Essence of the Sea Po'boy, 162
  It's Just a Grilled Caesar! Romaine Calm!, 58
  Krabby Patty, 138
Lightning-Fast Mini Meatloaves, 151
lime
  Chili-Lime Crema, 150
  Essence of the Sea Po'boy, 162
  Freestyle Fries, 118
  Houston! We've Got Huevos!, 30
  Jerk-Seasoned Chickpea Tacos with Pineapple Slaw, 148
  Simply Sublime Rice with Cilantro & Lime, 192
  Son of a Peach, 212
Linguine Aglio e Olio, 169
liquor. *See also* wine
  Son of a Peach, 212
  Tropical Contact High, 208

M

Make It Snap! Blistered Peas, 184
Make You Horno Pasta al Forno, 144
Mama Michaela's Cappuccino Yogurt, 42

ABOUT CANDICE HUTCHINGS

CANDICE HUTCHINGS is the face of the popular Edgy Veg YouTube channel and blog, where she delivers plant-based recipes with comedy and attitude, and the author of the best-selling *The Edgy Veg: 138 Carnivore-Approved Vegan Recipes*. She disrupts the vegan community with her candid and humorous takes on activism not only for animals and plant-based food but also for mental health, the environment and female empowerment. She lives in Toronto, Ontario, with her pack of rescue dogs.

▶ https://www.youtube.com/edgyveg

◉ @edgyveg

⌾ pinterest.com/theedgyveg

f facebook.com/theedgyveg

For more recipe inspo and videos, visit her at www.theedgyveg.com